MY DOOR-TO-DOOR SEARCH

FOR THE SECRETS OF WEALTH

IN AMERICA'S RICHEST NEIGHBORHOODS

RICH
LIKE THEM

RYAN D'AGOSTINO

LITTLE, BROWN AND COMPANY

NEW YORK BOSTON LONDON

Little, Brown and Company
Hachette Book Group
237 Park Avenue, New York, NY 10017
Visit our Web site at www.HachetteBookGroup.com

First Edition: January 2009

Little, Brown and Company is a division of Hachette Book Group, Inc.
The Little, Brown name and logo are trademarks of Hachette Book Group, Inc.

The excerpts from SkinnySongs by Heidi Roizen on page 226,
copyright © 2008 by Heidi Roizen, are reprinted here by permission of Heidi Roizen.

Library of Congress Cataloging-in-Publication Data
D'Agostino, Ryan.
  Rich like them : my door-to-door search for the secrets of wealth in America's richest neighborhoods / by Ryan D'Agostino. — 1st ed.
    p.   cm.
  Includes index.
  ISBN 978-0-316-02146-3
  1. Rich people — United States.   2. Wealth — United States.
3. Millionaires — United States.   I. Title.
  HC110.W4D34 2009
  332.024'0100973 — dc22   2008015328

10 9 8 7 6 5 4 3 2 1

RRD-IN

Printed in the United States of America

For Sarah

CONTENTS

GOOD PEOPLE TO KNOW

How I Met Them, and Why You Should Too

The woman stared at me, eyebrows raised, waiting. I was standing in the airy living room of her waterfront home, a stranger who had knocked on the door. In the driveway: an Audi A6. In the kitchen: golden oak cabinets, tooth-white beams overhead, and tawny hardwood underfoot, all absorbing the cold morning sunlight that skipped off the water and through the picture windows, as if this room was where the sun belonged. In my hand: a $1.79 steno notebook.

This was Westport, one of the wealthiest bedroom communities along what's known as Connecticut's Gold Coast, for the prevalence of extremely rich people and its location on the gentle shore of Long Island Sound. It is, in fact, the forty-third richest ZIP code in the United States, as measured by benchmarks including income, net worth, and home value. Paul Newman, Martha Stewart, Michael Douglas, Harvey Weinstein, and Michael Bolton have all lived there or still do. Presidential candidates swing through town for fund-raisers. The residents enjoy exclusive access to a pristine beach, a marina, and a golf course. On every parcel of waterfront property sits a home whose appraised value would cause many sane Americans to weep in bewilderment. Very nice place, Westport.

She looked me up, then down. She was around fifty, slim and blonde with clamshell-blue eyes; she wore a white cable-knit sweater. The morning news from CNN murmured almost inaudibly from a large flat-screen television in the corner. She clutched a coffee mug with both hands and leaned against the kitchen counter.

"Okay," she said. "What do you want to know?"

It was an appropriate question. There I was in this nice lady's living room, a writer who had come in from the cold. Through the bay window, I saw, at the end of a long deck that was built out over her beach like a boardwalk, the brackish waters of Saugatuck Bay sloshing around in a winter wind that whipped the tops of waves into foam. The sun bounced off the water, glamour-lighting the whole scene.

About a minute earlier, I'd stood in her driveway, gawking at the house — a towering A-frame with round windows that looked like portholes on a ship, on a tooth of prime shorefront property. My blue blazer, which held in its breast pocket my uncracked notebook and fresh pens, shielded little of the winter chill. I had gone without an overcoat deliberately — I figured the colder I looked, the greater the odds were that strangers would usher me into their homes. I was going door to door, and once I was in I could ask them what I yearned to know: how they came to be rich enough to live in such magnificent houses. More to the point, I was eager to understand how people build fortunes in America. How do they approach big decisions in their lives? In their careers and in their finances? How do they overcome missteps? How do they save, spend, enjoy, invest? How do they get *here?*

My wife and I like to take walks, especially when we're in a new town — for a wedding, maybe, or on vacation. Whenever we wander into a neighborhood of bigger, more beautiful homes on sprawling lots, invariably one of us asks, thinking out loud, only half serious, "Why don't we get to live there? And who does?" In Charleston, South Carolina, we once walked along the Battery, which cuts between the mighty antebellum mansions and the harbor. In Grafton, Vermont, we ogled farmhouses whose yards backed up to untamed woods. And in Seattle, we took a ride in a seaplane, nudging each other at the sprawling compounds that stud the islands of Puget Sound. We try not to point or drool. We don't begrudge the unseen nabobs who live in these tastefully landscaped homes. We dream. We think, *Wouldn't that be fun?* We're genuinely curious how they did it. We wonder if there's anything we could be doing better, smarter. We joke about knocking on doors, seeing what advice the home owners have, what they might tell us over a drink.

So, I decided to do just that — to introduce myself to dozens of people, all over the country. My day trip to Westport represented the first test of a hypothesis I hoped would teach me the secrets of wealth: if I knocked on enough doors in enough preposterously rich enclaves, I might gather enough insight and guidance to help me — and you, and anyone else who reads this — understand how to get rich; rich like them. Simple as that.

. . .

There are, of course, ways to go after this kind of information without traversing the country and ringing the doorbells of every mansion in sight. You can interview people who know a lot about investing, for example. Financial experts. Or you can read biographies of people like Cornelius Vanderbilt and Bill Gates—probably not a bad idea, actually. But no one had ever done it my way, so I was guaranteed information that was completely new in the pantheon of financial journalism. Which is cool. What's more, my interview technique was so unorthodox that, by definition, anyone who decided to participate had higher-than-average odds of being worth your time reading about. Why? Because close-minded, unadventurous, uninteresting people wouldn't invite a stranger into their homes and share their life stories with him.

I have to tell you, I got some strange looks as I stood in all those doorways. I was invading, after all. Politely invading, but still invading. I was knocking on the door and saying, in effect, "Tell me who you are. This is your home, presumably bought with money you earned. Tell me how. Take a few minutes to stand here in your well-appointed foyer and tell me how you got it. Off the top of your head, the first thoughts that come to mind. Tell me about your successes, your failures, your good decisions, your bad decisions, your insecurities, your pride, your children, your mentors, your first job, your confidence, your values. Tell me. Why? Because you could inspire a lot of people, starting with me."

Obviously—because you are holding a book in your hands—people told me a lot. Some people, anyway. The response to my interview ambush exceeded all expectations. On that first day in Connecticut, I knocked on thirty-two doors. At twenty of the homes, there was no answer. At six houses, housekeepers answered; each of them smiled and seemed bewildered by my presence—I can't blame them. One man feigned interest and promised he would call me later but didn't. And five people invited me in. Five out of thirty-two. A success rate of nearly 16 percent. That would prove to be higher than my overall rate, but not by much.

All in all, I traveled to nineteen towns in eleven states and walked close to sixty miles. I knocked on approximately five hundred doors. Of those five hundred, about half weren't home or didn't answer. Of the remaining two hundred and fifty, my official estimate is that housekeepers answered fifty doors, a hundred and fifty people declined to be interviewed, and fifty people talked to me—a success rate of 10 percent. Most of those fifty are included in this book.

When I met these people, I was occasionally served coffee or soda or water. I played with clinging dogs while attempting to take notes, drank twenty-dollars-a-glass Chardonnay with one of the richest women in Arizona, sped through the moneyed streets of Silicon Valley in a Ferrari, and ate a corned beef sandwich prepared by a CEO's private chef. I tailed a UPS deliveryman around Beverly Hills, slipping through driveway gates behind him. In Seattle I accompanied a woman as she walked her dog in the rain, and in Cleveland a retired chief executive officer showed me his collection of nineteenth-century English paintings. In Chappaqua, New York, I tried to chat up a Secret Service agent who was guarding Bill and Hillary Clinton's home. Those were a tense few moments: Sunny day, cul-de-sac, black SUV parked menacingly at the tip of the driveway, bull nose out. An intercom call box sprang from the lawn by the curb, like a sound box at a drive-in. My finger was an inch from the button when a man appeared on the lawn. He popped out from behind a tree, I think, although it happened so fast I couldn't be sure.

"Help you?"

I smiled and asked if anyone was home, stammering through my routine.

"Nobody's home," he said.

That's too bad, I said, because they could really give me some great perspective I won't get from anyone else, you know what I mean?

The guy looked at me, hard. Everything about his demeanor suggested that he was considering killing me at any moment, probably with one hand. Something might have rustled in the bushes just then, or maybe I imagined it.

"Nobody's home," he said again, his voice like a stone now.

I didn't say anything for probably five seconds — way too long for his liking, it seemed. I thanked him for his time and backed away. He disappeared.

I had a method. I had strategies. The basics are worth explaining.

My spiel: In my pitch, which started out extemporaneous but became polished over time, I said I was a journalist working on a story about the people who live in whatever town I happened to be visiting. I said I was traveling to affluent ZIP codes, *just like this one,* across the country, showing up unannounced, and walking door-to-door in search of people to interview. To demonstrate that I was a legitimate writer, or at least working writer, I mentioned my day job. My employment at a reputable publication always seemed to put people at ease.

Because this project would require so much flying around, and because I only had so much time and money, I couldn't afford to stay very long in any one place. I took red-eye flights, rented the tiniest compact cars, and made free coffee in hotel rooms. I determined up front that focusing on wealthy ZIP codes would be efficient; I could pinpoint my searches, fairly certain that every house I saw would belong to someone with a lot of dough. Why? ZIP codes tend to be large, and ZIP codes generally don't care how much money you make. They were introduced in 1963 to assist with mail delivery, and they can include people of any background. If a ZIP code lands on a list of the hundred richest, it means that somebody—and probably many people—within its boundaries has done something right.

My whole premise was that people who live in large, expensive houses must know something about making money. This is a generalization, of course. Once in a while, sure, a door opened and some rich guy gave me a few minutes of his time but had no real wisdom to share. Not everyone who makes $1.6 million a year is Lao-tzu. I had my trials out there, no question. Demoralizing stretches of gray suburban asphalt lined with empty, unfriendly houses. Then someone would finally open a door and offer a few bland aphorisms, not even trying. Or, worse, someone would bristle at my question and close the door quickly and not a little rudely, leaving me chastened as I retreated down the front walk, sure they were peering out at me through the window like I was some kind of proselytizer.

I couldn't feel wronged at such moments, could I? It wasn't exactly fair, what I was doing—surprising people by showing up at their door, and usually on a Friday or a Saturday. But when the rejection got bad, when the frustration set in and the blisters on the balls of my feet threatened to pop in my sweat-dampened dress shoes, I would always tell myself: wisdom is out there. And sure enough, it often seemed that whenever I was at my most dejected and hopeless, within the next five to seven houses I'd find a friendly, intelligent person who was happy to talk all afternoon. And that made everything okay again. Except the blisters.

I'm sure I could have learned a lot about success from the thousands of Americans in the next hundred richest ZIP codes and in the next hundred after that. But for consistency's sake, I stuck to my list of the top hundred. To find the wealthiest places, I had called one of the leading companies in the field of geographic information system technology, a firm called ESRI, which is based in Redlands, California. Basically, and for my purposes, it's a demographic research company. ESRI agreed to compile a list of ZIP codes by wealth, using criteria such as average and median household income, home value, per capita income, disposable income, and net worth. Atherton, California, was first on the list, and at number one hundred was Cabin John, Maryland. The ZIP codes on the list represented sixteen states. (The complete list appears on pages 231–33.) I spread my travels around geographically, to hit as many corners of the country as I could. (The list changes a bit every year. When I began my research, the 2005 list was current, but all statistics in this book are from the 2007 list. The sole exception is Austin, Texas, which missed the list by a hair in 2007.)

I did break away from the lists several times. The first was a stop in Sausalito, California, where I went one afternoon after canvasing nearby Atherton. I met an elegant, ambitious woman who owned an art gallery, lived on a houseboat, and had knowledge to share.

I also made a special trip to Las Vegas. Why Vegas? I couldn't resist. Not for the gambling, the strip clubs, or the all-you-can-eat buffets. (Although I do enjoy all-you-can-eat buffets, with their incongruous presentation of food glistening in Sterno trays: crab legs near the French toast, chocolate cake over by scrambled eggs, fruit salad adjacent to the roast-beef carving station. All for $14.95.) I went to Las Vegas because the city has experienced unprecedented growth in the past decade—new money mixing with old money mixing with no money. New residents, new businesses, new residential developments, new buildings downtown, new casinos on the Strip, new ideas. I knew I could find successful people there.

A third deviation was to Shaker Heights, Ohio. It doesn't show up on ESRI's list, but whenever I told people I was heading to the Cleveland area, that's where they *assumed* I was going. My actual destination was Gates Mills, a few towns farther away from Cleveland, but at the end of a day there, I spent an hour in Shaker Heights, and I was glad I did. Similarly, in Washington State, I visited a neighborhood in Seattle proper in addition to Medina, the list maker.

My last sidetrack was on my home turf: New York City. As I said, ZIP codes don't discriminate, and Manhattan's most affluent, 10021, stretches from the $30 million homes near Central Park to the inexpensive, one-bedroom walk-ups of Yorkville. These pull the average income down, but I still wanted to knock on those $30 million doors.

All in all, in alphabetical order by city, I traveled to:

ATHERTON, CALIFORNIA 94027

AUSTIN, TEXAS 78730

BEDFORD, NEW YORK 10506

BEVERLY HILLS, CALIFORNIA 90210

BRIARCLIFF MANOR, NEW YORK 10510

CHAPPAQUA, NEW YORK 10514

GATES MILLS, OHIO 44040

LAKE FOREST, ILLINOIS 60045

LAS VEGAS, NEVADA 89109

MEDINA, WASHINGTON 98039

NEW YORK, NEW YORK 10128

PACIFIC PALISADES, CALIFORNIA 90272

PALM BEACH, FLORIDA 33480

PARADISE VALLEY, ARIZONA 85253

SANDY SPRINGS, GEORGIA 30327

SAUSALITO, CALIFORNIA 94965

SEATTLE, WASHINGTON 98122

SHAKER HEIGHTS, OHIO 44120

WESTPORT, CONNECTICUT 06880

Walking a few miles through a town on a regular day tells you a lot about its rhythms, the cadence of its goings-on, its values, even its history. Knocking on strangers' doors reveals a town's fiber, its small glories, its rust and dents, its quiet spots. I met next-door neighbors who didn't know each other, and, in one town, good friends who lived miles apart. Throughout, I resisted the temptation to draw some tidy conclusion about any town based on the few people I spoke to. Anything like that would be inaccurate.

Also, a few times I took advantage of opportunities to interview a successful person even though I didn't happen to ring his or her doorbell. Sometimes, at the end of a day, I'd head to a local restaurant that had a bar, order a scotch and some dinner, and sit until someone interesting landed on the stool next to me. I did a few interviews that way, and several others occurred away from people's homes. In four instances, I chatted with people at their places of business: a bookstore, the art gallery in Sausalito, and two office buildings. I interviewed one guy only on the phone.

I did not carry a tape recorder. Instead, I wrote down every word in spiral reporter's notebooks, which fit neatly in the breast pocket of a jacket. (I've been reporting long enough to have developed my own method of writing shorthand—a Sanskrit mess only I can read.) I didn't attempt to record interviews because I probably would have landed fewer of them. It was challenging enough to get people to talk to me at all. If I had then shoved a tape recorder in their faces or even set it discreetly on a coffee table, many of them, I think, would have declined or would have spoken less freely. So, usually, it went like this: A minute or so into our conversation, I would politely say, "That's very interesting, what you just said. Is it okay if I write it down?" Once the notebook was out, any tension or awkwardness usually dissipated. I don't know why. Perhaps because our roles were now clear: Interviewee, interviewer. Talker, writer. Teacher, student.

So, what did I learn on my travels?

The answers are in the rest of this book. Generally, I found that there is no secret, fail-safe recipe for success—but, then, I already knew that, and so did you. I learned how to make smart decisions, how to work with people, how to work alone. I got tips on running a business, buying and selling land, saving and spending. Mostly, I learned how to think. The people I met inspired me. And I think they will inspire you.

Here is what else I learned about the people who get to live in dream houses: The people who get to live in dream houses are just people. Like you. The ones I met came from blue-collar backgrounds or moneyed backgrounds or somewhere in between.

They were proud, modest, eager to talk, reticent, skeptical, flattered, patient. Like you, maybe. They were cooking dinner, watching television, rushing to go pick up the kids, relaxing in the backyard, working—doing the things people do on Fridays and Saturdays, the days I did my walking; doing the things we all do.

Some had worked corporate jobs for their whole careers. Many had started and run businesses—sometimes after leaving a corporate job in which they felt cramped. All of them had worked hard, and most continued to. Even the few I met who had inherited their money worked hard—at not blowing it, at making it multiply, at proving that they too had ambition.

I should tell you what this book is not and what it will not give you. It is not a self-help book, but that just means it's not what you think of as a traditional self-help book. It is a book about what you can learn from people who have made a lot of money, but it does not include tips on picking stocks or estate planning or saving for college. Those are all worthwhile subjects, but I chose instead to look at the context of these lives, to tell people's *stories*. Some of their stories might inspire you to rewrite your own.

Here are some of the types of lives you'll find in the pages that follow, people who prove that by altering your view of the world you can achieve the kind of success that might always have seemed to exist only on the other side of some huge sheet of cellophane that you couldn't break through.

THE VISIONARY. The travel industry is not often thought of as a hotbed of innovation. But a few decades ago, Arthur Tauck, now in his midseventies, had an idea that would, in a way, revolutionize his small, family-run travel company in Westport, Connecticut.

(The idea is revealed on page 29.) Today, Tauck World Discovery is a pinnacle of the industry. Tauck himself, on the day I met him, seemed perfectly happy staying put in his living room overlooking the waters of Long Island Sound. Through his story and many others in this book, you'll learn something about how to come up with a revolutionary idea of your own.

THE "LUCKY" ONE. In the late 1960s and early 1970s, a young stockbroker named Bob Grosnoff, who's now in his sixties, bet his future on an unorthodox method of lining up high-net-worth clients. For a few years, he worked at it for long hours, and his co-workers thought he was nuts. When those big-money clients finally began paying up, no one could believe Grosnoff's spectacular "luck," which has carried him all the way to a statuesque home with a view of Camelback Mountain in Scottsdale, Arizona.

THE WORKER BEE. Not many luminaries in the world of fine art hail from tiny Newport, Tennessee, but that didn't matter much to Rena Holman. She learned early on that even if you marry well, you can't count on financial security, so she became determined to always be in a position to survive on her own. To get there, she worked harder than anyone she knew. But not so much anymore—she's too busy enjoying her home in Palm Beach, where I met her.

THE CONNECTOR. Heidi Roizen, who was around fifty when we met, was, until recently, among the more powerful venture capitalists in what might be the venture-capital capital of the world: Silicon Valley. Whenever some young, eager MBA student with a business plan and a dream summoned the chutzpah to ask her if she had time for a cup of coffee to hear his idea, she usually went along. Why? Because of three of the most important words in business: *you never know*. Roizen recently left the VC world. After guiding, advising, and funding a generation of entrepreneurs, she's now starting a business of her own. Because, hey, you never know.

THE RENEGADE. Growing up in Chicago, forty-something Rich Miletic washed windows and changed lightbulbs at apartment complexes where his father oversaw the maintenance. Miletic enjoyed patrolling the buildings by himself, fixing things, and he would later seek that sense of autonomy in his professional career. This pursuit of independence eventually took him on a solo mission to set up a business in Hong Kong and, after that, to Silicon Valley, where he owns a company and lives in the richest ZIP code in America. He was packing for a ski trip the day I appeared in front of his house, but he took a break to tell me, in his view, how to know a smart risk when you see one.

Most of the people who spoke to me seemed to have charged through life, operating on the theory that infinite possibility exists in the unknown. That's why they bothered to talk to me at all, I think. Some guy shows up at your door, tells you he's writing a book about success, and wants to pick your brain. Why do you agree to tell him your story? Why do you agree to tell him anything? There is no real, obvious gain in it for *you*—a person trying to enjoy a Saturday afternoon. Why do it? Why share your personal history, your beliefs, the maxims about money and hard work that you'll pass along to your children?

Why? Two reasons: First, because maybe you're a little proud of your accomplishments, and it's nice to be asked about them.

Second, you talk to the writer because you never know where it might lead. I sometimes wonder if this book you're holding might play a role in the creation of a wildly successful new business. Maybe it will bring two people together in some way— someone will feel inspired to take a chance and make that phone call or send that e-mail that's been a long time coming. (If this does happen, please let me know. And if you do become wildly successful and want to throw me a little something, I won't turn it down. I'm just saying.)

In telling the stories of the dozens of people I coaxed to the front door, I have made some effort to provide context and to tease out the lessons, but I also leave it to you to extract whatever guidance or wisdom you see—whatever speaks to you—and to be inspired by these people in your own way. They inspired me, each and every one of them. They are good people to listen to. I know. I've seen their houses.

ONE

OPEN YOUR EYES

To Connect the Dots That Lead to Wealth,
First You Have to See the Dots

Awe, then confusion, then elation.

That's the emotional continuum you speed along when you meet a certain species of rich person—the kind who seems to be just like you but with one difference: he had a great idea that made him enough money to build the towering house with the resplendent foyer in which you are now standing.

You're awestruck with admiration at first. *Wow,* you think to yourself. *This house is amazing. This guy must have it figured out. Is that a real Picasso?*

The confusion creeps in next, because the person is, or at least seems, pretty normal. Friendly, bright, but no more or less deserving of wealth than you. And you think, *Huh. Why him?* He tells you about the brilliant idea that afforded all this. *Good for you,* you want to say. *I guess some people are just lucky.*

Then you think about it a little more. A little deeper. And — wait a minute — suddenly there is clarity. A final, exultant sensation grips your cranium. Wealth is possible! Not money-making for its own sake — that's relatively easy, particularly if you work a hundred hours a week at a corporate law firm or take steroids (or both) — but the kind of riches that come from the pursuit of happiness and dreams and fulfillment. Wealth is possible, you realize — for you. Rich people aren't that different. Many of them once *were* you: smart people with motivation and a few good ideas. You come to understand this by moving from the beautiful foyer to the kitchen, by sitting at the table and hearing the story of how this person started out just like you . . . and then had a big idea.

That conversation, at the table or by the fire or in the front yard, is what I hoped for in every town I visited. Each time the wheels of the plane smoked a new runway late at night — LAX, O'Hare, Cleveland Hopkins, Phoenix Sky Harbor, Hartsfield-Jackson in Atlanta, wherever — I double-timed it through the sleepy terminal, so quiet I could hear the B-flat hum of the fluorescent lights, to the rental-car counter. I couldn't wait to start knocking on doors the next morning. I wanted to be awestruck.

It is an enviable skill, the ability to come up with not just a good idea but a breakthrough. A game changer. But it's a skill, not a gift, meaning that it can be learned and practiced. Forget about some genetic talent for innovation — it doesn't exist. Put simply, squeezing a great idea out of your brain begins with getting a good angle on the moments that make up your life. In this chapter, you will read about people who had life-changing ideas, rang-ing from industry-altering business models to tricks for playing the real estate game. And you'll see that coming up with these beauties requires little more than alertness.

"Always be looking for opportunity." You've heard this before, of course: in movies, in TV commercials for small business loans. But without specifics, it sounds hollow. Tinny. If you'd met the people I met, you'd see that with open eyes you can actually get there—to that moment when an idea sparks up from hot flint inside your mind, after what might seem like endless trying. I met a lot of people who had felt that way, and they all had one thing in common: they set a goal, and they remembered their goal at all times—when they were mowing the lawn, watching TV, commuting to work, taking a shower, lying in bed, eating breakfast. *Always.*

When you do this, your mind becomes a kind of hangar in which you store lots and lots of seemingly random information: people's names, stray bits of conversation, a story on page A17 of the newspaper, a billboard message along the highway. It might seem like a pile of trivia, the dead skin of the everyday. But by viewing all things through the lens of your goal, everything and everyone you encounter becomes a potential contributor to the big idea.

Here's an example from *MBA Jungle,* a lifestyle and career magazine for business school students entering the working world, where I once worked. The article "Brainstorm by Yourself" listed the various ways in which a person could brainstorm more productively and efficiently alone than in the traditional group setting. It cited a technique used by Rolf Smith, a retired Air Force colonel, who in 1986 had led the U.S. military's first Office of Innovation. He went on to run the Virtual Thinking Expedition Company in Fredericksburg, Texas, a kind of basic-training workshop on creativity for corporate managers. Smith once brought a group of marketers from General Mills to the sprawling Mall of America in Minneapolis. (They weren't solo, but the technique is what counts here.) He set them loose in search of inspiration that would help them sell more General Mills products. At an electronics store, they noticed that shoppers tended to stop and look at the televisions displayed in the window, their attention apparently grabbed by whatever was in motion on the screens. Later, at a pet store, the shop owner told the group that when someone picked up and held a puppy, the odds increased that she would buy it. These two seemingly random observations resulted in an inspired idea by the team from General Mills: a Wheaties box that featured a holographic image. The picture appeared to be in motion as consumers walked by it in the grocery aisle, catching their attention, and the changing-angle special effect enticed them to pick up the box, increasing the odds that they would buy it.

Smith's charges weren't just wandering through the mall — they were looking for ways to do their jobs better. If you put yourself in that mind-set all the time, you'll increase your odds of fusing two random scraps of information into one breakthrough idea.

My advice: carry a notebook. When an idea comes, you'll want to remember everything that might help you execute it.

Don't Forget Your Goal — Even When You're on Vacation

"I'm just always looking for the last best place."

In the first long interview of my travels, I met a woman whose mind was always trained on one goal: finding beautiful, undiscovered plots of real estate, preferably on a body of water. It's what many people want but few actually find — unless, like Carole Reichhelm, their fixation edges toward fanaticism.

Westport is the perfect town for Reichhelm and her addiction to waterfront property. Among all the affluent bedroom communities outside Manhattan, a Westport address is one of the most coveted. In 2007 the median household income was $157,087, and the average home value was $1,032,553. The twenty-seven thousand residents' average net worth was $1,278,975. The schools are first-rate; the beaches are padded with white sand; the train ride to Grand Central is sixty-four minutes; and upscale boutiques mingle with Brooks Brothers and Restoration Hardware on Main Street. You can get a sweet, juicy corned beef sandwich at the venerable Oscar's Deli, established 1948, or hit the buck-a-slice pizza joint, where Paul Newman has been known to stop in. The town holds an important place in my heart: it's where I got my first job, as a reporter for the *Westport News,* a twice-weekly paper. It is friendly territory. I know its neighborhoods and leafy streets well, so I made it the inaugural stop on my tour.

While in Westport, I was reminded how fervid a place it is, full of people making a lot of money and giving off the energy of productivity. As I ate a sixteen-dollar steak sandwich at Tavern on Main, I overheard three powder-puffed ladies in their seventies debating, over apple tarts and ice cream, the virtues of various real estate markets:

"Anybody got any ideas about where to invest for future growth?"

"South Carolina's good. And Georgia—especially ever since UPS moved everything to Atlanta. But you really have to do an economic analysis and see what kind of business growth is going on."

"There's a lot of empty office space in Dallas."

"Mm-hmm."

Knowing nods all around.

I stood in Carole Reichhelm's sunny living room staring out at the whitecaps on Saugatuck Bay; she leaned against her kitchen counter clutching a coffee cup, staring at me.

"Okay, what do you want to know?"

I basically told her I wanted to know what I had to do to be able to live in a house like hers.

Reichhelm said up front that her husband had worked on Wall Street for forty years and that his income had been the largest contributor to their current blissful-seeming situation. She had run an aviation business, managing corporate aircraft. "[Our wealth] didn't really happen until recently," she said, glancing out at the water. "We worked our asses off."

The Reichhelms' enduring commitment to hard work allowed Carole to build another source of income that helped boost their earnings even higher, by taking advantage of her interest in identifying undervalued real estate. She has raked in significant dollars over the years—and continues to do so—simply by buying and selling waterfront property, often in places you wouldn't think to look for an unsullied chunk of prize land. Like Arkansas, for example. And Baja, Mexico. Her eye for value has proved uncanny, but only because that eye is always open.

All the waterfront acreage in Westport, Connecticut, was bought up and developed long ago, so Reichhelm has trained her brain to look for it wherever she travels, especially when she's in a place the real estate experts haven't deemed hot. "God only made so much waterfront," she said, waving an arm at the bay outside her window. A seagull hovered above her dock, fighting the wind. "It's not like He's making any more." (Unless you count global warming, I suppose.) She and her husband, George, bought their coveted tenth-of-an-acre lot in 1983 for $260,000, eventually tore down the house that stood there, and built a new home. These days, George, who is retired, raises oysters on a little beach out front and sails out of the Cedar Point Yacht Club down the street. "We wouldn't take two and a half million for this place now," Reichhelm said.

Good for the Reichhelms, you might be thinking, but isn't the game over for the rest of us? Isn't all the habitable, affordable waterfront property in the world gone? As it turns out, no. Not by a long shot. If you want to find your little patch of paradise, you simply have to reject the conventional definition of "prime waterfront property." It ain't Westport, Connecticut, anymore, for one thing. Reichhelm's ability isn't something she was born with. She's simply figured out a formula. She defines it in an easy equation: earth next to water, minus trendiness, plus FOR SALE sign. This is what she looks for, always, no matter where she is.

"When everyone is doing one thing, do the opposite. I mean, most people would think I'm crazy because of the fact that I'm still buying land at all," she said. (Our interview took place at a time when the rest of the country happened to be loudly declaring the imminent bursting of the real estate bubble.) "People think the real estate boom is over because the hot spots are down. I don't think so."

Like the best stock investors, Reichhelm looks to get in cheap on land that isn't yet desirable. That way she can scoop up more property for less money; and if a couple of investments flop, the one that succeeds makes up for them. For example: Parts of Mexico and Central America are popular these days, particularly with American retirees, and prices in especially hot areas throughout the region are becoming inflated. But Mexico is a big country, and Reichhelm had noticed recently that on a dirt road on the Baja peninsula, parcels of land with a hundred feet of Pacific shoreline were selling for $500,000 and less. When we spoke, she had just bought one for herself. Property values there had already tripled by the time she got in, but they had started so low that she still got a deal. And the prices are still climbing.

The United States is a big country too. Many real estate speculators were scouring the Gulf Coast for deals in the months following Hurricane Katrina. But in 2006 Reichhelm was enjoying a vacation with her husband, driving through Arkansas, of all places, and snapped up three and a half lush acres along the Cossatot River for $120,000. She wasn't in Arkansas looking for property to buy, mind you, but her search for good land never stops. She's a little like an off-duty cop who witnesses a purse snatching—she's still a cop, so she acts. As Reichhelm puts it, "I'm just always looking for the last best place. And it doesn't have to be the 'It' spot. The earlier you get in, the more money you're going to make."

A week after I met her, Reichhelm e-mailed me a Web site advertising a new residential development along a river in South Carolina, urging me to get in on it because the houses weren't built yet and the area was still relatively undiscovered. She also mentioned that she had been vacationing in Belize recently and was investigating some stunning waterfront lots there that were selling for less than $100,000 each.

For many people, real estate is scary. For Reichhelm, it's fun—looking for hidden treasures, getting good deals, and turning over the parcels to eager homeowners at a profit. But it's only enjoyable because she learned how to do it and has practiced. When I was eight, I learned how to mow the lawn, and at first I didn't have any idea what I was doing. I sweated through each Saturday morning, pushing the awkward, heavy contraption around the yard, worried about shredding my mother's flowers, cutting the grass too short, and mowing my foot. But once I got the hang of it and got stronger, I looked forward to mowing. I hooked my Sony Walkman onto my shorts and listened to Red Sox broadcasts. I made twenty bucks a lawn in the neighborhood. I came to love it because I had confidence and experience.

Acumen like Reichhelm's can, in fact, be learned. There is skill involved, but it's skill you can develop by starting small. Has she been lucky? Only in the sense that she has gambled on a few out-of-the-way places that have become popular. (So far, none of her purchases have been total busts. The closest she's come to failing was a rental home she bought in Colorado that she wishes she'd held onto longer because its value kept increasing after she unloaded it.) And if, for example, the Baja deal turns out to net her a big profit, it won't be dumb luck. She will have set herself up to be lucky by finding those dots—quality land, a little tough to get to, offered at a low price—and connecting them in a way that made her money. And if the value of the land tanks, it won't ruin her. "If I go spend a couple hundred thousand dollars in Mexico, I have to be in a position for it to go badly and for the investment not to be in good shape for ten years," she said. In other words, successful experimentation with bizarre real estate transactions—or any business deal—requires that you stay within your means.

Reichhelm roundly exemplifies the traits that British researcher Dr. Richard Wiseman ascribed to lucky people in his 2003 book, *The Luck Factor:* "They are skilled at creating and noticing chance opportunities, make lucky decisions by listening to their intuition, create self-fulfilling prophecies via positive expectations, and adopt a resilient attitude that transforms bad luck into good." (More on how to create your own luck in chapter 2.) In one experiment, Wiseman asked two groups of people—one whose members described themselves as generally lucky and one whose members said they were usually unlucky—to count the photographs in a newspaper. The unluckies spent several minutes flipping through and carefully counting the pictures. The lucky people knew the answer in a few seconds. How? On page two, Wiseman had inserted a printed message in two-inch-tall type: "Stop counting: There are forty-three photographs in this newspaper." The lucky people, always on the lookout for unexpected good fortune, spotted it right away. The unlucky people, whose minds are usually closed to such signs, missed it completely.

Where Others See Death, Imagine Life

"I had a vision and a dream that people would buy something that they had not yet experienced."

Carole Reichhelm lives on a spit of shoreline, a few hundred acres square, cut off from the mainland by a narrow canal; I had accessed the small fantasy island by walking over a footbridge. A sign next to the bridge identified the neighborhood as private, but no one seemed to mind my strolling around and knocking on doors. After I left her house, I walked farther out, past the small Cedar Point Yacht Club and onto a street at the mouth of the Saugatuck River, where the homes sat on larger lots and faced Long Island Sound. I felt pretty good after my chat with Reichhelm—at least the day wouldn't be a total loss. Good. But I wanted to find another house quickly. The winter sun was hanging as high as it could, but the wind tore around my hands and up my sleeves and down my neck. I hoped the cold would make me look pathetic enough that someone else would let me in.

A few houses later, it apparently worked. An older woman answered the door. She didn't say much, but she seemed to regard me with compassion and motioned me inside. The home was contemporary and built virtually on stilts—you entered on the basement level and walked up a flight of stairs to the living space. The woman led me to a cavernous great room overlooking the water and invited me to sit at a dining table as long as a high school hallway. Through the bay window I saw that it was low tide; just beyond the front lawn, a pockmarked sandbar spread, between the house and the sound, like the surface of the moon. The thick windows sealed out the noise of the wind and churning waves, and the warmth inside the house stung my cheeks. After a minute, a tall man who looked a little like Donald Sutherland strode in, pulled out a chair across from mine, and sat down. I asked him my opening question, and he let a silent moment pass before speaking, his long, elegant fingers folded on the table.

"I don't know if you've ever seen a mill hole," he said in a pebbly voice so deep it seemed to come from somewhere under the floor. His name was Arthur Tauck; he was seventy-four years old when we met, and he ran Tauck World Discovery, a travel company based in Westport. He was explaining a lucrative niche he had discovered in the mid-1970s, one of many innovations that had come to him over the years as he transformed a local firm started by his father in 1925 into a travel industry leader.

He continued: "A mill hole is a hole in a glacier formed by water on the surface. It can go down three hundred feet, with water running down in, spinning like a flushing toilet. You throw a rock down a mill hole, and you think it's gone, and then after a minute, a long minute, it hits the bottom."

I told him I had never seen a mill hole, and he frowned, looking mildly disappointed.

"Well, we would take older people, in their seventies, and put a rope around their waist so they could crawl right up to the edge, on their stomachs, and look down into the mill hole," he said, raising his eyebrows ever so slightly, a kind of what-do-you-think-of-that look.

And this, in a way, is how Arthur Tauck made his fortune—by noticing opportunities. One long-ago winter, after taking over his father's modest tour company, Tauck was helicopter skiing in the Cariboo Mountains of western Canada. On that trip, he found himself wondering if anyone used the helicopters and remote mountain lodges during the summer. Turned out they sat idle. So Tauck contracted to lease a few fourteen-seat helicopters and open a lodge, sharing the costs of organizing, staffing, and marketing with a local business. Within months, his company began taking groups of mostly senior citizens to the Mendenhall Glacier, near where the provinces of Alberta and British Columbia converge—the kind of place his customers never could have seen had Tauck not embraced his moment of clarity. Glaciers, mill holes, and mountaintops with thousand-mile views. For Tauck and his clients, it was wonderful. "There are no roads," he said.

"We have three lodges, and you have to get there by helicopter. There's not one living soul up there."

Heli-hiking, he called it. A new form of luxury adventure travel. He had seen the lodges, looked at the glaciers, perhaps remembered an older client back in Westport who still had a spark of adventure left—all these pieces of information were stored in the hangar of his mind. And because he had the singular goal of trying to improve his business—all the time, wherever he was, whether in the shower or at the grocery store or on a chairlift three thousand miles from home—his brain was able to sort through and find the pieces that fit together to form the idea. Lots of people—even, it's likely, Tauck's competitors in the travel business—had seen those same lodges and helicopters in western Canada, but only Tauck thought to inquire whether they could be used during the off-season. Only Tauck came up with the wild idea of heli-hiking for old people. Granted, he was in the travel business, so it would seem natural for him to be constantly on the lookout for new trips and ideas. But that's the point: it was natural because he made it his nature. Whatever your goal, only by keeping it at the forefront of your mind *all the time* will you develop the ability to connect dots that other people don't. Arthur Tauck is proof that the world will never run out of good and profitable ideas.

This particular brainstorm was very clever but also a little crazy. Senior citizens messing around in helicopters and sliding across glaciers on their bellies? "I had a vision and a dream that people would buy something that they had not yet experienced," Tauck told me. "That was a risk! Does the seventy-five-year-old spirit still want to feel twenty-five years old? I thought so."

The heli-hiking trips have been booked solid for years, and they inspired Tauck to dream up other off-the-beaten-path itineraries. From his time in the Air Force, he knew that on old European road maps, yellow lines indicated less traveled—and more scenic—roads; today his "Yellow Roads of Europe" trips are among the company's most popular. When Tauck took over the business in 1958, there were two thousand clients and six different trips you could go on, all on the East Coast and none involving yellow roads or mill holes. These days, Tauck World Discovery serves tens of thousands of travelers each year and runs about 130 different trips to sixty countries and six continents. In 2006, President George W. Bush presented Tauck with the Preserve America Presidential Award, for his work advocating sustainable, environmentally responsible tourism.

Think about how you could do what Tauck did. What do you see every day? That hulking shell of a warehouse sitting empty, off the highway on the way to work. That vacant storefront downtown, near the park. Who do you know? Relatives, friends of friends, your kid's soccer coach. What do these people do? Is anyone you know starting a business? Looking for work? Interested in something you're interested in? If you can train your mind to look for undiscovered territory, you stand a chance of finding it, but it isn't easy. As Alex Osborne, the legendary advertising executive who coined the term *brainstorm,* once said, "It is easier to tone down a wild idea than to think up a new one." The key is to keep looking. Try writing a little note, like "The world will never run out of good ideas. What's mine?" and taping it to the bathroom mirror. That will remind you to always have your eyes open.

Carol Dweck, a psychologist and professor at Stanford University and a prominent researcher in the fields of personality and social and developmental psychology, studies the connections between people's outlooks and their likelihood of taking risks. "[T]he view you adopt for yourself profoundly affects the way you lead your life," she writes in her remarkable book, *Mindset*. Dweck identifies two types of people: those who have fixed mind-sets and those who have growth mind-sets. Fixed-mind-set people believe that they were born with a certain unchangeable level of intelligence, and they constantly strive to convince the world of their brilliance so that no one finds out they're not actually geniuses. Growth-mind-set people, on the other hand, believe that intelligence, knowledge, and skill need to be "cultivated" by trial and error—and that they can *learn* to see connections in the world. Failing at something, they believe, is the best way to ensure they'll succeed at it in the future. A growth minds-set, the very asset that led all the strangers I met to talk to me, creates a huge web of possibilities in your life: jobs you might get, romances you might encounter, investments you might snag a piece of, world-changing ideas you might have.

Dweck created an experiment to demonstrate how persistence in the pursuit of knowledge leads to success. She gave a series of trivia questions to a group of people with fixed mind-sets and to a second group who had growth mind-sets. After each answer, 1.5 seconds passed before participants were told whether they were right or wrong, and another 1.5 seconds passed before they were given the correct response. During this process, each person's brain was monitored with electrodes, which measured its reaction to the various pieces of information. Dweck found that the people with fixed mind-sets cared a lot about whether they were right or wrong but not at all about what the right answer was. Once they found out they had answered incorrectly, they tuned out. The growth-mind-set participants, meanwhile, stayed focused until the correct answer was given, revealing an interest in learning rather than in simply validating their intelligence. When the same trivia questions were asked again later, only the growth-mind-set group performed better.

When You Hear Someone Say "If Only I Could . . . ," You're Hearing an Opportunity

"It's hard for doctors to come home and work a businessman's day after working a physician's day. That's where I come in."

About half the people I spoke to around the country had started their own businesses. Of those, I would guess that 100 percent had growth mind-sets, which explains why they were able to come up with the one thing every successful business in the history of commerce has in common: a great idea.

Isn't that what business values most? Isn't that what brings in money? *Ideas?* Make hamburgers very quickly and sell them cheap. Sell your software programs only as a bundle, so people have no choice but to pay for things they don't need. Build a theme park with rides and hire people to dress up as the animated characters in your movies. Modernize Dubai. All of these were original ideas that reaped unprecedented rewards. Were the people who hatched them geniuses?

Let's say you don't want to be a billionaire. Let's say you just never want to have to worry about money again. You want to live in a nice house with three dishwashers (why not?), send your children to good schools, take nice trips, and generally live a sweet life. You just need one good idea.

But let's say you're, I don't know, a hospital administrator. You don't have tons of disposable income with which to assay

uncertain entrepreneurial schemes or alluring business proposi-
tions. You know from your line of work that the health care industry has a lot of flaws, and while you have no interest in going
into medicine, per se, you'd like to continue to work in a health-
related field.

Let's say you've noticed that medical specialists — ophthalmol-
ogists, radiologists, orthopedists, you name it — who work in hos-
pitals often feel hemmed in by an institution's bureaucratic and
administrative limitations. A single doctor at a smaller care center
could offer the kinds of services a hospital doesn't, and on a more
individual, personalized level. Eye doctors could open Lasik cen-
ters. A podiatrist could open an office that gives the most skilled
and specialized foot care in his city. Many doctors dream of this
kind of thing.

And these doctors, with their dreams of specialized care out-
posts, have money — often enough to set such a project in motion. And they have knowledge. But there's one thing they don't
have: time.

Mark Banta noticed all this, and that's how his idea was
hatched. I met Banta on a newly developed street in Austin, Texas.
The street itself probably hadn't existed a year before: twenty-four
one-acre lots, most with new houses popping out of the freshly
tamped topsoil, many of them for sale. On some lots, only the
very first scratching of earth hinted at a five-bedroom house that
would soon appear.

On the Saturday of my visit, an armada of late-model cars
was parked in front of the new mansion next to Banta's for an
open house. I parked here, mixed in. I shambled around on the
sidewalk trying to look casual, eyeing Banta's house to see if anyone was home. Banta, who wore faded jeans, a white golf shirt,
and a baseball cap, stepped out from behind a gate and walked

out to the street to check his mail, one of his three young sons tagging along. I introduced myself, said my thing, and he led me back up the driveway and through his remote-controlled gate. We stood chatting outside his garage as the boys blew up rafts for the swimming pool and lobbed a basketball at a hoop.

"I'm in the doctor hand-holding business," Banta told me. "I saw that the success of a hospital was based on patient admissions. Over time I realized that working at a hospital often just meant going to meetings all day. Managing the chaos. And the fact is, patients *don't* have to go to a hospital to have an MRI or a CT scan or a lot of other things. I quickly learned that a hospital is really a tertiary care center. People need primary care. There were holes in the care delivery system, and doctors knew how to fill those holes—outside the hospital setting. Which is where Banta Health Care Services comes in. I help doctors fill these holes better, faster, and more profitably than a hospital can do it by doing all the nonmedical things that are required in setting up a private shop—the logistics, the business-side part. See, it's hard for doctors to come home and work a businessman's day— finding a site for a new office, doing all the things that come with starting a business—after working a physician's day caring for patients. That's where I come in—the hand holding. I don't have to have the ideas, which is good, because I'm not that creative. And the beauty is, in the doctors you have a board of directors who are also your bankers. It's great."

In other words: Let's say Dr. Green is an ophthalmologist at a huge hospital downtown. Because of inefficiencies created by the hospital's bureaucracy, a simple cataract procedure takes more than an hour. If he had his own ambulatory surgery center, he could do five of these procedures in the same amount of time using a specialized team, modern instrumentation, and better anesthesia, all at a lower cost and with a higher level of safety. He would never have to request special permission from the hospital's administration to use a certain medication because it's not on a preapproved list. Dr. Green dreams about such a facility, maybe just outside the city, where patients can receive treatments more efficiently, without having to set foot in the huge hospital. He has access to the money to begin such a project, and he has the medical know-how to get it off the ground. But Dr. Green is so busy that he doesn't have the time to actually do it. Banta's company helps to secure funding, find real estate, manage staffing, set up participation by insurance plans, meet regulatory requirements, and everything else necessary to get a small medical business up and running. He can even manage the facility to make sure its goals are met each month.

"Everyone has forgotten that the patient is still the consumer, and that's the reason we're here to help," Banta wrote me in an e-mail a few weeks after we met. "Why not do it right? Also, many large organizations have forgotten manners. Private entities can be extensions of the doctors' personality and professionalism. People enjoy that."

Apparently, business is great. I was leaning against his 7,300-square-foot house on a prime lot in a new subdivision in a new development in a family-oriented ZIP code, where the average home was valued at $967,290. The home's architecture was Texas-Tuscan style — grand without being showy. A fountain sprang up between a front gate and the house's airy entry. Even the wooden, barn-style garage doors were beautiful to behold. And the kitchen did, in fact, house three dishwashers, plus two Sub-Zero refrigerators and a Wolf range.

Banta was genuinely proud of the place. "I just wanted the home to be livable and fun for the boys, not too formal," he said.

"Like a little country club for them. We put a pool in the back, we have big yards in the front and back, an audio/video play-room — the boys even have their own garage for scooters, bikes, dead frogs, bugs, and the other cool stuff they like to keep."

He wasn't boasting, and he pointed out that most people he knew in Austin made an effort to downplay success and wealth — money was for enjoyment and security, not display. "You have a lot of seven-figure folks, and you also have a lot of eight-figure folks too. You just wouldn't know it. They wear blue jeans and golf shirts," he said. "I just traded my Mercedes — I had five of them, actually; I was really into German cars for a while — and bought a Ford pickup."

When I asked him whether he had been this laid-back when he was revving up Banta Health Care Services, he insisted he was. "I was single at the time. Fearless. Being single was nearly re-quired. A young wife is not real excited about you working seven days a week, fifteen to twenty hours a day, traveling for fifty days straight, and risking it all. A single guy can sit on boxes, doesn't need drapes or cable TV, can eat hot dogs for breakfast, and doesn't need or have the time to spend a lot of play money. Money will come later, in a big way. Delayed gratification! There is noth-ing to lose when you are young and single with great ideas, an MBA, and a willingness to work like your father told you to. If you fail? Or fail again? Or even again? Your penalty is to go get a W-2 hospital administrator job, get a nice title for your business card, and drink coffee all day while going to board meetings. I would rather own a junkyard."

Connect the People You Meet

....

"If I made a list of all the things in life I thought were coincidences and then looked back at them, I would see that they weren't coincidences at all."

....

I needed a place to stay in Beverly Hills. Despite the notoriety it received through the eponymous early-1990s teen television drama that my younger sisters used to watch, Beverly Hills 90210 is only the sixty-fourth richest ZIP code in the country. It has a median household income of $149,195, the average value of a home is $1,216,175, and the residents' average net worth is $1,250,635. Still, not too shabby.

In every town I visited, I tried hard to experience, just a little, what it was like to live there. I sought out the new restaurant the locals were checking out. I talked to bartenders and store owners and taxi drivers about their customers. But because I was on a budget (unlike the people who actually lived in these towns), I also experienced what it was like to stay at the La Quinta Inn out by the airport.

Which is exactly the kind of room I was about to book when a friend who lives in Los Angeles mentioned that she had a connection at a place called Raffles L'Ermitage. I, the prole, had never heard of it. I looked it up online, and my jaw hit the keyboard. L'Ermitage is generally considered one of the finest hotels in the world.

I weighed my options. Budget motor lodge by the airport or one of the finest hotels in the world? No disrespect to the good people who operate the La Quinta chain, but I went with L'Ermitage. My friend helped me get a special rate, and, just like that, my new hosts afforded me the treatment appropriate for someone trying to experience the Beverly Hills lifestyle. When I pulled up in my economy rental car, three men in suits greeted me: one parked the car, one took my bag, the third held the door. (There may have been a fourth, ready to step in and perform any additional tasks. I'm not sure—the curbside arrival was a bit of a blur.) There were chocolates, *good* chocolates, and some little palmiers in the room. There was a king-size bed, a forty-inch television, and a sweeping view of the hills that give the town its name. In the cavernous bathroom I found a telephone by the toilet, the kind of handy touch the rich are always thinking of. Between the bed and the walk-in closets was a stretch of elegant lattice paneling made of English sycamore; I half expected a geisha to pop out from behind it. I put a Charles Mingus CD into the stereo system and stepped out onto the balcony. I was getting into character.

I met Harvey Jason, a rare-book seller, on my second full day in 90210. The sun broiled the hilly streets I had been walking up and down all afternoon, and I felt molten. My feet throbbed in my black lace ups. I slung my sport coat over my shoulder, sick of wearing it. My *hair* was hot. I deviated from the residential rows for a while, wandering in search of air-conditioning down Sunset Boulevard, where the Hustler store and greasy Duke's diner sit within walking distance of $6 million homes.

One of my biggest weaknesses in life is used-book stores. Wherever I go, whatever town I find myself in, if I see one, the whole afternoon is shot. If it's a large, well-stocked shop, after an hour I'm just getting warmed up. I don't always buy a lot—sometimes nothing—but then that's not really why I'm there. I just like books.

On Sunset Boulevard, I found a great store. Two, actually, but the first, a large store called Book Soup, was closed for renovation. I stood for a moment, bummed, staring blankly through the door. I turned to leave and noticed a small sign pointing down a skinny alley: MYSTERY PIER BOOKS, it read. The name sounded vaguely *Harry Potter*-ish to me. The alley led to what turned out to be an oasis of pristine first-edition books, and there I would encounter one of the most pleasant and inspiring characters in all my travels, Harvey Jason.

Mystery Pier is housed in an outbuilding about the size of a one-room schoolhouse, tucked behind the larger storefronts on Sunset. I was rocking on my feet, scanning the shelves in the first of two rooms, when Jason popped out from the back. He was over five feet tall but far from six, and had closely cut graying hair, a neat goatee, and a smooth, proper British accent. From his first words he was exceedingly polite, affable, and easy to talk to. He smiled and gave his usual invocation: he sold only first editions, which were arranged by type in various sections of the store — true crime, poetry, fiction, biography, and a few others.

Jason went back to busying himself at a small desk in the rear room, and I browsed for five or ten silent minutes. I made my way back and saw handsome display cases where, behind glass, Jason kept his most prized holdings: dozens of first editions by the likes of Hunter S. Thompson, Truman Capote, Raymond Chandler, and Ken Kesey — many of them signed by the authors.

Jason asked if I was from the area, and when I explained what I was doing in town, his face brightened and he half whispered a long "wowww." *Either he is genuinely intrigued by my project, or he's a good actor,* I thought. I would soon find out that he was both.

· · ·

I've given a lot of thought over the years, as most people have, to what I would do if I had enough money to do whatever I wanted. I think I'd open a bookstore. Jason was living a dream we both shared. Not long into our conversation, I had the idea to include him in what I was writing. Why not? I asked him if he happened to live close by, and, sure enough, he and his wife lived in a house just above Sunset Boulevard (very nice). Their home was not technically within the borders of 90210, but it wasn't much more than a football field away.

He pulled up a chair for me, and we talked for more than an hour, pausing only when a phone call or a customer came in. After just the first few minutes I understood why Jason was so willing to chat with me — and why his business was so successful. To him, every stranger was a potential source of friendship, business, or, at least, interesting conversation. He talked about gratitude and the important role it had played in his success. He saw his own good fortune as a by-product of his relationships, both professional and personal, with other people. Nurture those, he said, and good things will come. For Harvey Jason, the people he had met in his life became the dots he connected. "If I made a list of all the things in life I thought were coincidences and then looked back at them, I would see that they weren't coincidences at all," he said.

Jason's previous career was as an actor, and with his looks and manner he could easily play the part of a soothsayer who lives deep in some mossy forest; he's a slim man with a soft voice that inflects with an unusual mix of wisdom and curiosity. After three decades of acting on television and in the movies, Jason decided in 1996 that he was ready to ease into a retirement gig. He was in Eureka, California, of all places, filming Steven Spielberg's *The*

Lost World, in which he played a dinosaur tracker, when he had the revelation that he would finally go after what he wanted in life. Jason had visited a local bookstore and was examining his purchases in the common room at the Carter House, the Victorian-style inn where the cast and crew were staying during the shoot. "That evening, a group of us were sitting around, and I was thinking about the books, and I thought, That's what I want to do. I looked at Steven and said, 'I'm going to open a bookstore. I'm going to do it!' " Jason loved acting, but something about that shop in Eureka convinced him that it was time to pursue a different dream.

Jason was fortunate to have bought his current house in the hills long ago (out of probate court, no less, for $150,000 in 1972; it is now worth nearly $3 million), and he earned royalties from syndicated TV shows. Still, when he opened Mystery Pier—a joint venture with his son, Louis, who was already a bookseller specializing in mystery novels—he couldn't afford to lose money on it.

The budding entrepreneur came up with two ideas early on that helped differentiate his shop from others. One was to specialize in fine first editions, which, he hoped, would tap the lucrative collectors market. "Two weeks after the store opened, somebody called looking for some Faulkner—*Absalom, Absalom!* or *A Green Bough* or something. And I thought, That's where the money is," he said. Not exactly revolutionary, as he'll be the first to point out, but it gave him some hope of profit.

His second big idea came not long after, and it has transformed his business and his life. As both a movie buff and a Hollywood veteran, Jason thought it would be fun—and, who knew, maybe even profitable—to dedicate a corner of the shop to books that had been made into films. A genre encompassing other genres. Jason and his wife, Pamela Franklin, an actress who once died on-screen in Marlon Brando's arms in the 1968 film *The Night of the Following Day,* knew a lot of people in the movie business, and Mystery Pier's collection of handsome copies of "books into film" caught the attention of Hollywood's elite. "I was a writer and an actor, and I had various contacts from doing that kind of work," Jason told me, an understatement. "So we began to get requests for books that were to be given as gifts—from the people who put on the Emmys, then from the Oscars, and from various directors and actors. It was all fortuitous. The success of this part of the business was sort of inadvertent. My son says we invented a new category of literature."

The niche grew even bigger. Before long, Jason's client list included Robin Williams, Jude Law, Michael Caine, Bono, and Spielberg, all of whom would stop in for first editions. Jason focused more attention on bolstering his Hollywood collection, even seeking out writers to autograph books they had written and directors and actors to sign the books of movies they had directed or appeared in. Among the treasures I saw the day I visited were a full set of the Harry Potter books signed by J.K. Rowling ($40,000); Humphrey Cobb's *Paths to Glory* inscribed by Kirk Douglas ($6,500), who appeared in the film version; and a copy of *Leaving Las Vegas,* by John O'Brien, signed by Nicolas Cage, who won an Oscar for his performance in the film ($5,500).

"Word just got around," Jason said, shrugging. Here, I believe, is why word got around: For starters, Jason was a remarkably dependable utility player, and his acting résumé is long. To share a few highlights, Jason appeared in the 1973 film *Save the Tiger* (an excellent movie for which Jack Lemmon won the Academy Award for best actor, beating out Jack Nicholson, Al Pacino, Robert Redford, and Brando); *Judgement: The Trial of Julius and*

Ethel Rosenberg, a 1974 TV movie in which Jason played Roy Cohn; a 1976 TV miniseries called *Captains and the Kings* (his all-time favorite job); *Air America,* a 1990 film starring Mel Gibson and Robert Downey Jr.; and what sounds like every TV show ever made—*Batman* in the 1960s; *Sanford and Son; The Streets of San Francisco; Police Woman; Hawaii Five-O; Charlie's Angels; The Love Boat; Wonder Woman; CHiPs; Trapper John, M.D.; Knight Rider; Family Ties; Night Court; L.A. Law; Picket Fences; Seinfeld;* and many more.

Television shows cycle through guest stars every week. Actors show up, film their scenes, and go on to the next thing. But Jason was good, and his personality was memorable, and he became well connected. That wasn't necessarily his goal—it's not like he went through his career dealing business cards and shaking hands because he wanted to build a network that would fuel his hypothetical bookselling business one day. No, he was simply kind to people. He made his on-screen career primarily as a character actor who would steal a scene here and there—a good guy to have around. Off-screen he was also a good guy to have around because of his kinetic vibe of genuine optimism, gratitude, and warmth. I'm convinced that "word just got around" about his bookshop because of who Harvey Jason is: a good storyteller and a kind man. He is *interested* in people.

Jason's networking success may have been accidental, but he nonetheless built what Stephen Garcia, a social psychologist who teaches at the University of Michigan, refers to as social capital. "Meeting new people can be a reinforcing mechanism that helps you improve your standing, although that might not be—and probably is not—the goal in and of itself," Garcia says.

Veteran financial journalist Jason Zweig, an admitted lover of unsentimental data and empirical evidence, nonetheless considers stories like Harvey Jason's to be solid proof of the value of personal connections. In his fascinating book *Your Money and Your Brain*, Zweig explores the emerging science of neuroeconomics, a blend of psychology, neuroscience, and economics that seeks to better understand what drives our financial decisions. "I'm an empiricist and a skeptic," Zweig says. "There's something very mystical and New Agey about this that bothered me when I started the research for my book, but the evidence is there. And if you think about it, it makes sense: success in business and success in life really are a function of who you know and how many people you know."

Zweig told me a story about an inadvertent networking triumph not unlike Harvey Jason's. A few years ago, a major publishing house Zweig had never worked with offered him the coveted job of writing the biography of an important economist. After Zweig turned in the manuscript, the editor in chief of the publishing house told him how pleased he was with the final product. "We'd never met or even spoken; he was just moved to call me and tell me that. Very nice of him," Zweig says. "So we're chitchatting, and then it occurs to me that I don't actually know how this all happened in the first place, and I say, 'You have to tell me something: Why did you guys ask me to write this book? You know, of all the gin joints in the world, how come you called me? Why wasn't it Joe Schmoe?' "

The editor told him that a few months before he called Zweig, he had been having lunch with another journalist whom he told about the project, lamenting that he couldn't find the perfect writer. The woman immediately said, "There's only one person you should ask: Jason Zweig."

As the editor recounted this story, Zweig thought, *I'll be damned.* He realized what had happened: The woman who had referred him was one of Zweig's former colleagues, and he had seen her at a party not long before her fateful lunch with the editor in chief. Normally shy, Zweig nonetheless had felt the desire to "linebacker" his way through the crowded room to say hello to the woman, whom he hadn't seen since she left the company. "I didn't have an ulterior motive. She was somebody I hadn't seen in a while and who I like, and I wanted to catch up with her. Now, did she later recommend me to that editor because she really thought I was the *best* person in the world to write the book? I'm sure that was part of it. But the real reason was that on an impulse, I had taken the time to go talk to her, and we had a nice chat, and so my name was on the tip of her tongue. And I'm sure if I had not crossed that room, she either would have given them three or four names, or she would have said, 'I don't know; let me think about it.' But she said my name only. I have no doubt that that's why it happened."

Harvey Jason, the bookseller, has been crossing rooms his whole life, also with no ulterior motive. "If we're happy, we make people happy. If we're miserable—well, you know how contagious misery is," Jason said, sitting at his desk at Mystery Pier, leaning back in his chair. "Gratitude is the single emotion that propels me through life. It's the only emotion, I believe, that is thoroughly incompatible with negativity. And without negativity, you can have optimism—and optimism creates more optimism. I look over my shoulder and say, 'This happened because of this and this and this.' Today I'm an optimist, but I'm an optimist based on my own experience."

Even When You Find the Sure Thing, Save Some Money for a Rainy Day

....

"Most of the millionaires I know lost their first million. Why? Because they wanted the big office and the big car and everything."

....

Las Vegas is one of only a few places I visited that is nowhere to be found on the list of America's richest ZIP codes. Still, I felt I needed to go there. People had been flocking to the city for years in well-documented waves, bringing with them the human energy needed for an economic boom. The average annual growth in the population of Clark County between 1990 and 2006 was 5.6 percent. And in the final four years of that long boom, from 2002 to 2006, the median home price leaped from $159,800 to $317,400, according to the National Association of Realtors. So I knew the city had lots of new people and lots of new money. Still, Vegas seemed a strange place to me, and I didn't know what I would find.

One longtime resident compared the relationship between Las Vegas the destination and Las Vegas the city to that of Disney World and Orlando: the locals grudgingly appreciate its presence as a source of jobs and revenue, but they never go there for recreation. The Strip exists as a kind of amusement park, and it's not something most locals seem to consider part of their lives. If they work there, it's a job, nothing else. If they don't work there, it's just the street where the nice restaurants are. What struck me was how quickly you can leave the Strip behind. Drive a few miles north, and the incandescence suddenly dims to a normal, large-town/small-city level. You see street lamps, gas stations, veterinary offices, pharmacies, people walking dogs—the humdrum of suburban modernity, only in this context it seems surprising and strange.

Some of the houses nestled between the main drags were spectacular: austere relics from the time of the city's birth juxtaposed with monolithic testaments to its recent growth—lots of good knocking, it looked like. But, as it turned out, after spending one full day walking endless sidewalks through several of the city's long-standing neighborhoods of wealth—which were only about forty or fifty years old, I guessed—I was left wondering whether I would find anyone to talk to at all.

The reason? Gates.

I should have been prepared for this. Before I traveled to any new city to knock on doors, I always researched its neighborhoods, its real estate trends, its wealth distribution. I needed to know where to knock to reach the filthiest of the filthy rich. One handy technique I used frequently was to study the Web sites of two or three high-end real estate brokerages in a given city or town, scan their online listings to find a few homes selling for astronomical prices, and punch in the addresses at Google Maps. These homes became the epicenters of my search; by piecing together walking tours through their neighborhoods, I was certain to find other expensive houses.

Google Earth, incidentally, was another asset to my advance work. If you haven't seen Google Earth, I recommend it. You can type in your home address—or any address or city in the world—and watch as a relatively recent satellite photograph of your house appears, often showing every shrub and deck chair. Yes, it's a little terrifying. But it's also a fantastic tool. Try typing in "Baghdad" or the address of the new house your sister just bought a thousand miles away, and you can see it instantly. Recently, my wife and I were thinking of staying at an inn we had found online, and we punched it up to see if it was as "secluded" as the Web site claimed. Lo and behold, just beyond the frames of the lovely photos on the site was a four-lane highway. Also, if you happen to be writing a book about rich people and you want to check out a particular neighborhood in a town you've never visited to verify that you'll be walking among estates with swimming pools and that those estates are not four unwalkable miles apart from one another, it's quite useful.

Before I went to Vegas, I thought I was fully prepared. Unusually well prepared, in fact, with a long list of multimillion-dollar street addresses in multiple neighborhoods. But one item that somehow eluded my due diligence was the gate factor.

For some reason, Las Vegas residents (they're called Las Vegans, it turns out) seem to enjoy the presence of large, electronically operated gates at the ends of their driveways or, more frequently, at the ends of their streets. And here's the weird part: Gates don't just guard the high-security palaces in ritzy subdivisions; you might expect gates there. They guard split-levels, ranch houses, and two-families on ordinary streets. Nice enough homes, but a gate? And some of the gates are actually manned by a person in a little hut who checks permits on windshields.

My first day, a Friday, was bad—the only day on any of my trips that I didn't meet a single person. I wanted that feeling I had when I got off the plane: possibility. Smart people, great stories. Instead, all the houses looked pale and sad to me, as if the people had moved out a year before. At the few doors I actually reached, no one answered. As night gathered in the sky, I thought of my little boy at home in New York, not even six months old. I missed him. I missed my wife, who was probably giving him a bath or warming some applesauce. I asked myself what the hell I was doing in residential Las Vegas, at some random intersection of latitude and longitude, walking down a street where nobody wanted to talk to me, my rented Chevy alone in a church parking lot a few blocks away. I looked down at the heartbreaking wrinkles in the pants my wife had pressed the day before, back in New York, and which I had feebly tried to touch up with the hotel iron; at my sport coat, buttoned, sharp; at my reporter's notebook tucked into the breast pocket, two new pens, in case one ran out, capped and gravid with blue ink.

Then I righted myself, drifted out of the doldrums. I almost said aloud, "Remember: This is a good idea, what you're doing. You've connected a couple of dots in your own life, haven't you?" The door-to-door salesmen I had seen in movies. The journalist I had become. A door-to-door journalist. Two dots, connected! It would work. I would make it work, because everywhere in America, some people were living their dream. I would find those people in this town too. To hell with the gates. Fortunately, I had scheduled two full days for knocking in Las Vegas, one of the only cities where I knocked on multiple days. The sun was setting on Day One. If Day Two was going to be any better, I would need some help.

That night, when I most needed comfort and fortification, I found it in a meal I will remember for a long time. A friend of mine works in restaurant public relations, and thanks to her I enjoyed three fine-dining experiences in Las Vegas that were so decadent that after I washed down the last bite of seared Kobe beef with the dregs of my Bordeaux on night three, I felt almost guilty. A culinary trifecta: Thursday at Joel Robuchon at the MGM Grand, Friday at RM Seafood at Mandalay Bay, and Saturday at Picasso, overlooking the fountains at the Bellagio, where

I ate seven courses immediately before boarding the red-eye back to New York (slept the whole way). It was staggering.

At the 16,000-square-foot RM Seafood, I sat alone at the bar. I ordered the tasting menu prepared by the chef and owner, Rick Moonen. The first thing to hit my taste buds after the long, fruitless day was a briny, juicy Kumamoto oyster topped with bursting paddlefish roe. Even the soft, chewy bread was a highlight, served with terra mouselata, an addictive, tangy paste made from pureed potatoes, carrots minced almost to invisibility, Monini olive oil (from Umbria—Moonen swears by it), and carp roe. Each course was paired with a wine, and by the fourth course I had loosened up enough to stop worrying about my day. While I ate, a steady parade of servers, cooks, hosts, and regulars huddled along the bar, creating a lively little salon. Parked as I was for more than three hours and with no obvious dinner companion, I waited for conversations to come to me, like the guy at a party who sits in one place all night while the action bounces off him—a bell in a pinball machine. Everyone was friendly, and many showed a keen interest in Project Door Knock, or at least enough interest to sustain a conversation for fifteen minutes.

Besides me, the one other constant that night was the bartender. She had lived in Las Vegas for many years, and throughout the evening she suggested streets and neighborhoods I could visit the following day, nooks where access to big houses might be easier. But many of the communities she suggested had proper names, which often indicated the presence of some ogre sitting at a post, opening and closing an entry gate. Queensridge. Spanish Trails. MacDonald Highlands. She couldn't be sure which of these were sealed off by fences and which weren't, so I planned to hit them all the next day, my last in town, and prayed that at least one of them permitted the hoi polloi inside. But it sounded grim.

Then, lightning struck, in the form of a man two seats down from me, who had been buzzing in and out of our conversation.

"You know, I live in Las Vegas Country Club," he said. He studied me, waiting for a reaction, until he saw that I was unaware of the significance of this fact. Las Vegas Country Club, he explained, was a gated community that included all kinds of housing: small apartments, high-rises, modest one-families, and large, expensive houses. Some of its carefully laid out, curving streets were lined with monstrosities that had been built in the city's early, gangbuster years. (In Martin Scorsese's 1995 Vegas mob movie *Casino,* someone later told me, the scenes at the home of Robert De Niro's character were filmed behind the LVCC gates.)

The man, who I won't identify so that he doesn't get kicked out of the LVCC, offered to give my name to the guard the next morning. "Once you're inside the gate, you're in," he said.

The bartender brought me the pan-seared barramundi with a rich hash of foie gras and sweet potato and a glass of 2004 Craneford Barossa Valley Grenache. Things were looking up.

Saturday morning in my room at the Bellagio, I was still buzzing happily from the previous evening's dinner when the guy from the bar called to let me know that the arrangements had been made for me to smuggle myself into the Las Vegas Country Club. I drove my rental down the Strip, past the convention center, and up to the LVCC barricade. Sure enough, a hefty, uniformed woman sitting in a hut handed me a placard granting me access for One Day. I shoved it under the windshield on the dash. It indicated that I was supposed to park only in front of my host's home, even though, technically—ha!—I didn't have a host. I drove with ex-aggerated slowness, trying not to look too eager.

The development was an impressive, elaborate complex of all kinds of dwellings, and I spent the next twenty minutes rolling through it at a crawl, getting my bearings. A fragrant golf course wrapped its way in and around the homes, a hotel, and an inordi-nate number of security guards scooting about, probably looking for illegals like me.

After my introductory meandering, I targeted a small hive of large homes on a few adjacent streets I could canvas without mov-ing the car. I had driven no more than five minutes from my hotel on the Strip, but the bing-bing-bing and clack-clack-clack of the casinos had dissolved, overpowered by the eerily hushed suburban stillness: no one outside, houses standing lazily, minia-ture people playing golf silently in the distance. I parked at the end of a cul-de-sac, out of view of passing security vehicles, my car blocked by a rambling, modern house that occupied the en-tire island in the center of the turnaround.

Behind the eighth door I knocked on, at the mouth of the street, I found Roxy Stutzman.

Actually, I found her college-age granddaughter first. Stutz-man's house, which sat on a corner lot and, like most in LVCC, backed up to a fairway, looked solemn from the outside. Oh, it was awesome—a rambling brick place raised up from the road, with complicated, expensive landscaping. But the shades were drawn, the front door shut tight behind iron bars. I rang anyway, and the girl opened up and peered out at me through the grate. I asked if the home's owner was available to tell me how he or she ended up living on such a lovely street, and the girl said, "My grandmother. She'll talk your ear off. Hang on." About a minute later, she came back, opened both the door and the iron gate, and ushered me into a dark, marble foyer. Walking away, she instructed me to wait there. I could hear Stutzman fussing around for something presentable to wear, bickering with the girl, who groaned. Two easy chairs, each covered with a mound of blankets, sat in front of a television, a tray table between them. DVDs and videotapes were stacked next to the TV, as if a child were home sick from school. Framed silhouettes, photographs, and small watercolor paintings of what looked like European cities hung in the darkened foyer. To the left, through French doors, a formal dining room was being converted into a billiards room, or maybe it was the other way around. Blinds blocked the view of the swimming pool outside (I later saw it on Google Earth). Stutzman appeared, and we settled into the two chairs.

"Marry the right person" was the first thing Stutzman said, as she sat down and smoothed out her robe. She had wispy, copper hair and fair skin that looked well protected from the Nevada sun. Her granddaughter sat in the kitchen nearby, occasionally looking in at us as her grandmother spoke. Stutzman continued: "Marry someone who either has money or is motivated to make money." But there was more.

Her husband had begun his career, probably like almost anyone else who moved to Las Vegas in 1970, in the gambling industry. He worked as a casino shift boss. "He tried to go forward in the gambling business, but he eventually had to get out because he wouldn't do anything illegal," Stutzman said. She said that he once produced a popular impersonation show at the Flamingo Hilton, which Stutzman assured me was the longest-running show in the hotel's history. At one point as she spoke of her husband's casino career, her granddaughter, having ambled in and arranged herself rakishly on the arm of Stutzman's chair, chimed in with a smirk that Roxy had once been a dancer, then giggled. I think it was a joke, but I'm not sure. Stutzman let the comment pass, and continued:

"My husband is a genius. But he's a practical genius. He never went to college." I asked if he was a particularly hard worker, and she nodded, saying, "He works with his *brain*."

Stutzman gave her husband most of the credit for their good fortune, but it was clear to me that she was an equally important half of the duo. She wasn't just his cheerleader. Her role, it seemed, was to be practical, to be the one with her head screwed all the way on, so she could step in and temper her husband's lofty plans when those plans became too much for their finances to handle. He, it seemed, had perfected the practice of always looking for opportunity, but when he saw one, he sometimes pursued it too aggressively. Roxy understood that the strategy works only when you protect yourself from the uncertainty inherent in trying to connect the dots in search of fortune.

"Most of the millionaires I know lost their first million. Why? Because they wanted the big house and the big office and the big car and everything. Don't overextend yourself. You have to have money to regroup. That means you can't have all your eggs in one basket. Don't get greedy. You just *can't* get greedy. Just take the profit, put the money in the bank, and go on to the next project. Greed and ego make you make mistakes," she said.

This might be advice you think you've heard before, but, let me tell you, this woman understood ambition, and she meant every word she said. The Stutzmans' resourcefulness had fueled whatever success they enjoyed, but she showed restraint and cunning. She has always tried to make mental connections, looking for ways to earn money that no one else will think of.

About my writing career, Stutzman, who said she was a published poet herself, offered this advice, nodding as she spoke: "You really need to write some trashy stuff first, like Harlequin romances. Get some money in the bank."

On looking for good, cheap real estate: "In my opinion, you have to get real estate journals on the Internet and find out where the hot spots are. Really do your research and find out things like where dams are going up, new roads, whatever."

On how to still get rich off the Internet: "Health care. Offer some health care service. People are living longer. The life expectancy up until 1900 was like fifty. But now . . ."

In the mid-1980s, Stutzman and her husband thought they had come up with a humdinger, a surefire way to connect two dots—downtown Las Vegas and Nellis Air Force Base, twenty minutes north of the city—that would make the couple some serious money.

"You know what an atom smasher is? It goes around the track, and it separates atoms into smaller particles," she said, making circular motions with her hand. She was referring to a particle accelerator, a massive machine used by physicists to answer questions about mass, matter, the physical makeup of the universe, and the future of the cosmos. "Well, they were talking about bringing one here, to Nellis. So, we bought land in North Las Vegas, between North Las Vegas and Nellis." She looked hard at me, almost squinting, nodding slightly—like, Get it?

The Stutzmans surmised that if the particle accelerator were built—it would have been the only one of its kind in the United States at the time, she said—it would bring jobs to the area, good, high-paying jobs, and those people would need nice places to live, close to the facility. Her husband had eased successfully into the real estate business after leaving the casinos, and they researched the area using his connections and knowledge of the local market. Then they acted quickly.

They disagreed about one major point: He wanted to sink the couple's entire savings into the plan, according to Stutzman. But Roxy, the voice of reason, set the cutoff point at one quarter of their holdings. He eventually relented, and they went for it.

And?

"Well, they didn't bring it here. I think it's in Texas," she shrugged. "But that would've been a coup. Ah, well. But we still made a lot of money, just because it was good land, and just the fact that they thought about bringing it here showed you what kind of growth we were having, even then," she said. "We made a *lot* of money."

In their own way, the Stutzmans did everything right. Roxy understood that nothing is a sure thing, so she insisted they wade in slowly. Still, the couple knew there was a good chance the investment would pay off, atom smasher or no atom smasher, because rumors of the project led them to what they discovered to be undervalued land. Their scheme had two components of success in real estate or anything else: the creativity necessary to see an opportunity, and the restraint required to limit losses if the opportunity falls short.

The investment was a big move, even after Roxy reined in her husband's grander ambitions. But you don't have to sink a quarter of your life savings into a speculative land deal to be a successful dot connector. You simply have to be able to see and think beyond the headline in the newspaper that says "Particle Accelerator May Come to Nellis." Ask, what could it mean for you? All around us, every day, are opportunities to make associations that others can't see. An idea for a new way to sell a product. A bit of creative networking—calling on an old friend who, what do you know, has a good connection that could benefit you in ways you'd never thought of before. The trick is to see all your options and then, once in a while, when you think you've discovered an in, to make a move. Carole Reichhelm, the woman in Connecticut who's obsessed with waterfront property, searches for parcels of land in the oddest places. Some people might have laughed when she told them she bought riverfront property in Arkansas. But because she had ample money to begin with and had already made a few moves that paid off, she can afford to take a flyer on each new prospect. The Stutzmans, meanwhile, stood on sound enough financial footing to be able to invest a quarter of their savings in a question mark. Even if all they ended up with was a bunch of real estate in a booming city, they couldn't lose.

Once You Connect the Dots, Follow Through

"I saw opportunity. It was a new area with a wide-open market."

British researcher Richard Wiseman's experiment — in which the people with open minds flipping through the newspaper saw the message "Stop counting: There are forty-three photographs in this newspaper" while others passed right by it — made me think of Rena Holman, an art dealer I met in Palm Beach, Florida. (Her story is told in more detail in chapter 4.) She got her start in the fine-arts business working for a Memphis man named Hugo Dixon, who had made his fortune in the cotton business. One of her more successful enterprises was the sale of fine kilim rugs, which are woven by hand primarily in Eastern Europe. Holman had traveled to Hungary and Romania in search of affordable art to sell to clients back home. She discovered the rugs, and they later became popular, which was good for Holman, who had the connections to get them. I asked her how on earth she thought to go to those places to look for art in the first place. "Well, Hugo had traded in those countries when he was in the cotton business, which led me to find out that these rugs existed," she said, matter-of-factly. Connection made.

That was an astute association on her part, but connection alone doesn't make a penny. It took a tremendous amount of energy for Holman to act on it. That's a key part of this business of seeing what others don't: the skill is valuable only if you actually do something about the connections you make. You can imagine Holman saying to herself, "Boy, I bet those people over in Eastern Europe who bought Hugo's cotton make some mighty fine rugs," and then going on with her day, never giving it second thought. But to fly to Hungary and seek out the artisans and then promote them back home and turn them into a significant part of your business? That's following through.

How does one summon the nerve to follow through on an idea? Sometimes by doing simple arithmetic. Holman would have calculated the expenses she thought would be associated with importing the kilim rugs, what prices she could sell them for, which of her clients would be interested—and just like that, she would have given herself a pretty good idea of whether or not to book that first flight.

A doctor I met in Las Vegas, Sohail Anjum, had made a similar calculation. I rang his doorbell on that hot day in the Las Vegas Country Club shortly after interviewing Roxy Stutzman. Underneath Anjum's ornate, bleached-brick house, large for its lot, was a gaping garage from which an SUV nosed out. Inside the house, I walked across the white marble that appeared to coat much of the largely open first floor. An exotic bird chirped in an old-fashioned cage. Anjum was dressed rather well for a Saturday.

Anjum had bought the lot twenty-two years before, around 1984, and had knocked down the previous house to build the current one. "We leveled it and built brand new. That was our best decision: making a home on this location," he said. "We thought about remodeling the original house, but then we would still be in an old house."

Before that, his best decision, he said, was to move to Las Vegas in the first place. He had attended medical school in Queens and done his residency in Buffalo when he heard about an opening in Nevada. "When I was looking at moving, there were two hundred thousand people here. Now there are four million. I saw opportunity. It was a growing city then, and it's still growing. It was a new area with a wide-open market," he said.

Then came the arithmetic and research into the housing market, the medical community, the weather. And then, feeling that he had discovered a true opportunity that many others might have passed over, he followed through. He *moved*.

Opening their eyes, recognizing what was in front of them, and acting on it. That's what everyone in this chapter managed to do. It's not easy, but anyone can do it. The final piece of that equation—acting on an idea—marks the point in the trail where the terrain gets a little tougher. Following through requires hard work, commitment, and all the other things we're told stand between us and the promised land. Doesn't always sound like fun. But in fact, once we discover something we love, something to motivate us to work harder—besides the boss's threats or a mountain of credit card debt—the "hard" part of the work melts away. We become driven by desire. We persevere—another word that does not connote mirth—but it feels less like work and more like . . . life. Why? Because instead of praying for a lucky break, we'll have challenged ourselves to meet a goal, and any feats required to achieve it will feel like what we were born to do, rather than something someone made us do.

In the next chapter, you will learn about people who were driven by a sense of purpose, which pushed them to sweat it out as they inched toward their goals. They got "lucky" in the end, but only because they spent years setting themselves up for overnight success. What's the most important lesson they can teach us about luck?

TWO

LUCK DOESN'T EXIST

How to Get Yourself One of Those "Lucky" Breaks Other People Are Always Getting

I saw Derek Jeter one morning in Scottsdale, Arizona. As a life-long fan of the Boston Red Sox, it is my natural duty to loathe and detest all things of or pertaining to the New York Yankees, and that includes Jeter, the team's shortstop since 1995 and its current captain. I hate him for every one of the twenty-three home runs he hit off Boston pitching in his career (as of this writing) and for the ten punishing runs he has knocked in during postseason games against the Sox; for being so irritatingly squinty eyed and clean shaven; for the superhuman diving catch he made in the roily summer of 2004, hurling himself like some mad mosher into the stands beyond third base, mutilating his face but snaring the ball somehow; and for playing with such histrionic determination and posting such ostensibly good statistics as to make you think he's better than he actually is. The poser.

But, of course—*aaack,* I can barely type the end of this sentence—Derek Jeter really is great. Phenomenal, actually. I've booed him many times from a safe distance at Yankee Stadium and Fenway Park, but I'd pick him first for kickball, no question. His determination is real, and he probably is an even better player than any of his career statistics would indicate.

And that catch—it still makes me shudder with disgust and admiration when I see it replayed on a highlight reel. In the twelfth inning of a game not halfway through the season—no championship on the line yet—Trot Nixon, Boston's right fielder, hit a fly ball foul, down the third-base line. Jeter ran as fast as he could, blowing past his feckless third baseman, Alex Rodriguez, to catch the ball, and couldn't stop himself from diving headfirst into the seats at Mach 2. Only after several deadening seconds did he emerge, hoisted back onto the field by the fans, propped up onto his feet by the trainer and his teammates, his eye swollen and bloody, his cheek already purple with rot, the ball in his glove. He had saved two runs.

And here's the thing: I don't think it mattered that it was the twelfth inning, that it was the Red Sox, or that he was on national television. It could have been a spring training game against the luckless Kansas City Royals—it's just what Jeter does. The reason, I think, is that he knows that if he doesn't make a habit of it during the regular season, his body might not remember how to do it again in October. And so when I saw him striding out of the Breakfast Club in Scottsdale, past the hipsters and the retirees, squinting, I didn't want to punch him, surprisingly. I realized at that moment that I respected him. And that's the nicest thing I'll say about a Yankee, ever.

Was it a lucky catch? For some players, it would have been. A fluke. But Jeter tries hard every time—doesn't know any other way—because he is driven by the idea of victory and perhaps by a fear of failure. He never stops trying. He has raw talent, of course, but who's to say a guy who pumps your gas or heads up the marketing department wouldn't be playing for the Yankees if he'd had the same drive when he played high school ball? Jeter feels purpose, and that makes him work. He wants to win. Doesn't every ballplayer? Not all of them as much as he does, I don't think. When the Yankees slump, I love it. (Wait—that's not how I meant to end that sentence. Let's try again.) When the Yankees slump, the New York sports media always ask Jeter, the captain, what's wrong. His response, consistently and to the frustration of any sportswriter looking for a good quote, is usually the same: we just have to keep going; we just have to play better; we just have to work harder. A boring, unsatisfying response yet utterly true.

The Breakfast Club, incidentally, makes a mean jalapeño biscuit.

The idea of making your own luck by working hard isn't new. My father likes to pull out the old maxim "Luck is preparedness meeting opportunity." It's the preparedness that's the tricky part. What does it mean, exactly? If you don't know what the opportunity is going to be, how do you prepare for it? The answer has something to do with twisting around your whole frame of mind. Work hard, and you can actually create the opportunities instead of waiting for them.

Before I wrote this chapter, I asked my father to tell me a little about perseverance. He is the hardest-working person on the planet. He grew up in a solidly blue-collar family—my grandfather was a welding foreman at Pratt & Whitney, the jet-engine manufacturer—went to a state university, then state law school, and eventually started his own practice. He ran that for a couple of decades before settling in at a large, successful firm that someone else has to run. Most nights when I was growing up, he would work at the kitchen table until midnight, a cup of English breakfast tea at his hand, tidy stacks of marked-up documents and yellow legal pads where dinner plates had been earlier in the evening.

I asked him what he thought the key to his own success had been. "I just worked," he said after a moment. That was true: He worked. Relentlessly. Every night. Sometimes weekends. The yellow legal pads, the cup of tea. The sound of the garage door rattling up in the morning while I still lay in bed—Dad's going to work. I have been thinking lately about what drove him. He would probably chalk up his perseverance to his Yankee heritage. The old New England work ethic, you know. Shovel your own snow. Change your own oil. Be frugal—you never know when you'll need that L-shaped scrap of plywood. It wasn't that he loved the law above all else—he would rather have been a farmer or a factory owner. But he excelled, so he seized it as a means to an end. And, now that I think about it, I know what that end was, what drove him: me, and my brother and sisters, and my mother. Everything he has done, he has done for our happiness. I envy his drive, but lately I think I've been feeling where he gets it. I've got a wife now, and a little boy.

But—as if to give his four kids a little more to emulate—here's the real trick my father pulled off: He did not, in fact, "just work." He made sure to remember why he worked. He was always around, home for dinner every night at 6:30. As a family, we took dream vacations—skiing in Idaho, sailing in the Caribbean, summers on the Connecticut shore. He would sometimes have to spend an hour on the phone, usually one of those 1980s "car phones," a giant beige brick connected umbilically to a battery pouch. But he was there nonetheless. He coached my basketball team at the Y when I was six. He took off work one afternoon to bring me to a hydroelectric power plant for a seventh-grade science project. He never missed one of my track meets in high school. Luck? My siblings and I are the lucky ones. My father knew the life he and my mother wanted us to have, and he knew that if he ever let up, he would risk not being able to provide it.

The result was that this blue-collar boy, who could rebuild a Volkswagen engine by the time he was fifteen and who paid his way through law school by driving a beer truck, is now among the top lawyers in his field in the whole United States. Lucky breaks can come out of nowhere, but he showed me that if you work as hard as you can and look alive (as he would say), you'll see and catch more of them. I'm sure there are many in his area of specialization who wonder how he got lucky enough to land all the good clients and be part of the biggest deals. Well, he spent a long, long time getting lucky.

You know what he told me? The real prize wasn't the clients or the deals. It was for my parents to be able to raise us kids the way they wanted.

Choose Your Purpose, and Don't Let Anyone Tell You You're Wrong

"After that call from the private plane, the guys in the office didn't tease me anymore. They'd say, 'How'd you do it?' "

It was fitting that just two hours after my Derek Jeter sighting, I met a man whose doggedness and perseverance led to a career filled with hard-earned luck in his own field, finance.

They were a long two hours, though. I was in the wealthy enclave of Scottsdale, Paradise Valley, ZIP code 85253, number sixty-three on my list. Its 18,890 residents enjoy (I assume) their average net worths of $1,356,956 and their lovely homes, which are valued at an average of $1,070,460. I walked and walked on level streets, hearing nothing but the dry breeze, meeting no one. The town's landscape was colored with a simple palette — copper, feldspar, lavender. My shoes pestled the edges of suburban desert streets into a fine dust that discolored my pant legs around the ankles. I kept thinking about the TV show I had seen the previous night in my hotel room, about people in densely populated neighborhoods in the American Southwest who had discovered rattlesnakes in their yards. I was uneasy.

Finally, I rang the doorbell of a modern-style home perched high on a corner lot, wreathed with saguaro cacti, mesquite, and bougainvillea. A woman who immediately reminded me of the actress Ali MacGraw answered the door. She introduced herself as Katherine Grosnoff, invited me in, assured me that her husband, Bob, would be glad to talk to me, and went back to arranging flowers in the kitchen.

I set my notebook on a black marble bar facing the open living and dining rooms. When Bob Grosnoff descended from upstairs, he showed me to the black leather chairs in front of the bar. Outside a wall of windows, Camelback Mountain took a bite out of the cloudless sky.

Trim, calm, and possessing a unique linguistic ability to speak in neat paragraphs, Grosnoff, sixty-six when we met, had become a stockbroker in 1969, near Philadelphia. As it turned out, that was a terrible time to become a stockbroker. The market seesawed all year, up and down, up and down. Was it uncertainty about the Vietnam War? Gas prices? The turbulent cultural climate in the

United States? Whatever the reason for the instability, Grosnoff needed a way to do better. He challenged himself to figure out the market.

He noticed that many potential big-money clients were showing caution: Business owners were selling their businesses and taking the cash. Instead of playing the market, which was making everyone nauseous, high rollers were buying certificates of deposit, which promised modest, but at least guaranteed, returns.

Grosnoff had an idea. It wouldn't be fun, and it wouldn't make him much money right away. But if he stuck with it, the payoff down the line—if the damn market ever shook off the heebie-jeebies—could be huge. Grosnoff began selling a better-paying (and safer, because they were backed by the government) alternative to CDs: short-term municipal debt that yielded 7.5 percent tax free. (These tax-anticipated notes with a federal tax deduction were available for a few years in the late 1960s and early 1970s.) It was a good idea that made sense to the buyers, but in a way it was no easier than pushing stocks because it required long hours of cold-calling and garnered a low payoff. "One of the earliest transactions I did was a five-million-dollar order. It had a two-hundred-fifty-dollar commission, and I only got twenty-eight percent of that," Grosnoff said. "It took about two hours to place the trade. So if you figured it out on a pay-per-hour basis, I was making a grand total of thirty-five dollars an hour doing a five-million-dollar trade."

Not surprisingly, he was the only broker he knew who was adhering to this plan. "No other brokers were offering these because the commissions were so low. The other guys would tease me and ask why I was spending two hours on an order that paid me so little," he said. "The other guys would say to me, 'What are you doing?' Because they would hear me cold-call people who had just sold a business, and I had a canned speech: 'You're probably buying CDs right now, but I have tax-anticipated government notes at seven and a half percent. I'll be in town on Monday, Tuesday, and Thursday. When would be a good time to stop by?' I'd tell them I was just starting out. The reason I did this"—which he didn't mention to the other fellas in the office—"was that I knew that when the market turned, the guy on the other end of the phone was going to buy IBM, and he wasn't going to just buy a hundred shares. He was going to buy a lot. So basically, I was lining up future clients."

That was the idea, anyway. It was risky, and Grosnoff spent hours, weeks, and months on it. He hoped that when the market did turn around—and it always turned around eventually—his new clients would remember that young Bob Grosnoff had surfaced during a particularly dyspeptic time in the history of the stock market and had heroically served up tax-free government bonds whose high yields had tided them over. He hoped that these people would take the money they had made during the hard times and invest in stocks—with Bob Grosnoff! It was more than hope that fueled him, actually. He believed in his mind that he'd figured something out, and he was out to prove it. To himself, his co-workers, whomever. It didn't matter who. It was a challenge.

The plan worked. After chasing the notes Grosnoff had scattered like chum for a few years, his new high-net-worth clients started calling when the market began to rise, and this time their eyes were trained on much larger transactions. No more little bonds. "My best day, probably, was when a coal miner—and by that I mean a guy who *owned* a coal mine—called," Grosnoff told me. "He said, 'Bob, get out your pencil. I want to buy some stock.' He started with the As, then the Bs, and kept going. When he got to Johnson and Johnson, the phone went dead. He called back and apologized and said, 'Sorry; I'm on my plane. Where'd we leave off?'

"After that call from the private plane, the guys in the office didn't tease me anymore. They'd say, 'How'd you do it?' "

Just lucky.

Grosnoff's self-awareness may be his biggest asset. He knew exactly how he got his reward. He didn't consider himself lucky at all, because he knew that the man on the plane didn't call him randomly. Bob Grosnoff knew that the only person he had to thank was Bob Grosnoff. According to Jason Zweig, author of *Your Money and Your Brain,* understanding and believing this—rather than seeing it as a one-time lucky break—was essential to Grosnoff's future success. "When people feel that they earned money through their own action rather than random chance, they will be much more confident," Zweig says. "You did it, it's on you, it's all you—and you just get these incredible feelings of love and trust about yourself. A particular part of the brain seems to become active when you feel that your action and effort resulted in something good: the caudate, which comes from the Latin word for tail, because it's sort of shaped like a tail. This is a basic circuit in the reward system of the brain. That feeling of having earned it through your own actions is processed in the same parts of the brain where you experience love and trust. It gives you a real warm glow—a different warm glow than you would get if somebody gave it to you. That doesn't feel bad either, but that's more of a surprising feeling. In this case, you feel, *yeah, I did it, and I'm great.*"

Remember: With Time Comes Free Money

"It's the miracle of compounding."

I never did see a rattlesnake in Arizona, thank goodness. In fact, my sole encounter with a hostile member of the animal kingdom, not counting a bitchy housewife in Beverly Hills, occurred within the borders of the tame, leafy town of Westport, Connecticut.

One rule I tried to follow in every place I went was stay away from streets marked PRIVATE. But I made that rule only after my brush with death in Westport. I am fairly certain that, by law, anyone is, in fact, permitted to walk down a private lane. Still, if a bloc of rich people is going to bother to post a sign at the end of their street asking people to keep out, they're probably not the type who will open their doors and welcome some guy who wants them to talk about their money.

Maybe I shouldn't have been surprised. These shores had a history of clashes between residents and intruders. On April 25, 1777, nearly two thousand British troops under the command of General William Tryon landed on what is now Compo Beach, on their way to raid the inland town of Danbury. They marched right down Compo Beach Road, burning everything in sight. About fifty local militiamen fought to the death trying to fend off Tryon's troops, but the British moved through the town like a tsunami.

And now here I was. It was late afternoon, and I was walking past a stretch of large houses on Compo Beach Road, along the water. I wasn't having much luck—the owners either weren't home or their gates were too high. Eventually, I spotted them: two women—a mother and her adult daughter, I guessed—

sitting in a round, glassed-in sunroom drinking tea. The house was Kennedyesque in style and status, with bay windows that looked out onto Long Island Sound. The women were examining some ugly, expensive-looking metal sculptures in a manner that suggested they had either just bought them or were planning to sell them. *Perfect,* I thought.

The problem was I was on the wrong side of the house, and the property was ringed by a stone wall. I walked up to the end of the block, attempting to flank the house from the back. At the top of a slope behind the inland side of the house was a private road, from which a driveway led, tributary-like, down to the house. I strode past the PRIVATE ROAD—NO TRESPASSING sign and saw the house through a copse of hemlocks. At the mouth of the winding driveway was a fenced-in tennis court, and there something caught my eye: a tail thumping the ground. An animal's tail. The tail of a large dog, in fact, who was standing sentry, glaring at me. It looked like a wolf—I guessed it was a cross between a Doberman and a German shepherd. I froze, and not three seconds passed before he darted away from me and disappeared into the trees on the other side of the court. I waited for a breathless minute and, not seeing the dog, gingerly continued on my way down the driveway.

Then—damn—I spotted him again. He was lurking in the trees not twenty paces from me, watching me like—well, like a guard dog. *Okay,* I thought. *Forget it. I can take a hint.*

But it wouldn't be that easy. This myrmidon was now walking slowly toward my position, his yellow eyes locked on mine. He was emitting one of those long, low, gutteral growls that are more menacing than the loudest bark. I was too scared to even mutter "Nice doggy." It would have been the perfect time to toss a raw steak on the ground and be on my way, like in the cartoons, but I managed to retreat backward, the way I had come, one careful step at a time. A kinetic silence crackled between us. He could have lunged and ripped me to pieces right then and there, and no one holed up in any of the awesome houses would have had any idea. He mirrored every step I took with two of his own. When he reached the edge of his master's property, he sat, gargoyle-like, waiting, until I had walked the entire hundred yards — backwards — down the private road.

After the incident with the wolf, I wandered around Compo Beach, the town park that offered ball fields, picnic areas, a marina, and a beach where, in the summer, nannies took kids to play, and high school cheerleaders flirted with lacrosse players. I walked across a field, white under the fading February sun, looking out at Long Island Sound, my eyes teary from the wind. Eventually I stopped at a large brown-shingled house that was separated from the beach by the road. As I approached the side door, an old, osteoporotic black Lab pushed hard against the asphalt to raise his heavy, lumpy body, one brittle leg at a time, and tried to muster a growl but ended up just wagging his tail and circling me, limping. I rang the bell, and a pug the color of bread dough went berserk on the other side of the door. A housekeeper appeared, smiled, held up her index finger, and disappeared again. I stood mumbling as amiably as I could to the Lab for a few minutes before a stylish blonde, midforties, strolled out into the driveway carrying a plate of chocolate-chip ice-cream pie. I thought maybe it was for me, but she started taking bites herself. I realized that she had company, apologized, and rushed through my spiel. At the time, I was working for *Money* magazine, which I mentioned.

"Money?" she said through a mouthful of pie, referring to

currency, not the publication. She turned and motioned to the house like a woman on a game show presenting a prize. "Ta-da!" She laughed a little maniacally and ice cream dripped off her lower lip. "My advice? Save money," she said. The pug was attempting to hump my leg. The woman took my card and said she would call me after her company left. I thanked her for what she had already told me, knowing I probably wouldn't hear from her.

I stayed on the beach road. The late-winter chill intensified as the white sun leeched the color out of the sky. I had time for one more house — good thing, because I didn't want to finish on such a weird note. At the opposite end of the beach, a sign at the mouth of a road read NO OUTLET. *Not* PRIVATE, just NO OUTLET. Handsome, mid-twentieth-century houses on majestic waterfront perches. This was my last shot.

One couple told me in a manner politer than necessary that they had just returned from a wake. Next door to them, an expansive house that looked like a European government building from the outside — beige, rectangular, with quoining at the corners — seemed unpromising. No cars in the too-big driveway, a single light on upstairs. But the bottom of the sun was already under water, so it was now or never.

"Come on in, come on in," the owner said. "I was just doing some work upstairs — my wife is away. Florida. I could use a break." He ushered me in through a foyer painted with decorative trompe l'oeil marble pillars. He wore a blue V-neck sweater and khakis and later told me that he was sixty-seven years old, but he looked younger. He had worked as the chief executive officer of several large corporations — in publishing and in the food and beverage business, notably — and asked that I not use his name. "I've learned that, for me, publicity is best avoided, if possible," he said, smiling. As I did with one or two other people I met who made the same request, I obliged.

Oddly, a white carafe of hot coffee, the kind you see in corporate conference rooms, sat on a small service cart in the corner of the living room next to a stack of Styrofoam cups. I accepted one (strong, bitter), and the CEO cracked open a caffeine-free diet Coke. He flicked a wall switch that ignited a gas fireplace.

"We paid four hundred and fifty thousand dollars for this house in 1979," he said, sinking into a sofa next to the fire. "Now it's worth nine or ten million. It's almost all original—we added on this room here, but that's pretty much it. What makes it good is its location. See—and this is what I tell my kids: it's the miracle of compounding. Save early. It works with money, and it works with real estate. Now, you might say to me, 'Why don't you sell this place and pocket the money?' Residential real estate in a very good location is the best investment there is. And the truth is, I do think about selling it."

At its core, that wasn't a conversation about real estate or investments. He was giving me a lesson in patience. By definition, stick-to-itiveness (which is actually in the dictionary) takes a while. When it comes to most projects, you don't "stick to it" for six months. Now, this guy was in a no-lose situation after he bought the waterfront house, but his point was valid: there's a time and a place to cash out, but the trick is not to leave any money on the table—and, perhaps more important, not to leave any enjoyment on the table. A good friend of mine is currently mulling the idea of selling a beachfront house he inherited, to get through a patch of financial uncertainty. Only trouble is, he has this vision of his children's children sailing along the shore, the way he used to with his grandfather—and that vision, I *think,* is going to keep him from going through with a sale.

Through the glass walls of the CEO's living room, we watched the top of the sun turn fluorescent orange, like the suns in cheap Japanese paintings of Mount Fuji. The sky became a deep, peacock blue, on its way to black. He took a swig of soda and looked out the window, opened his mouth to say something, and then stopped. Then, after a few moments, he said softly, "This is a magical place."

My advice to you after meeting this man: pit logic against what you believe. Logic might dictate that you should sell your house or change jobs because you need a shot of money now, but think past tomorrow and think past the next day. Think about ten years from now. You'll have earned ten years of unbeatable financial returns, and you'll have accrued ten years of memories in the house. That's far down the list of definitions for *perseverance,* but it's an important one.

Watch Your Pennies, No Matter How Many You Have

"I have a lot of friends who are one financial mistake away from disaster. What you have, you hang on to for a reason."

Earlier that day, across town, I had met a woman whose home would also be considered a magical place by many, although it was far more modest than the CEO's. Still, waterfront in Westport is waterfront in Westport. The house was sheathed in gray shingles. A white wooden swing, the old-fashioned kind built for two, hung on the front porch, the better to gaze over the rock seawall at the reedy beach and the bay beyond. I rang the bell, and after no one answered I started toward the next house. I was halfway there when a BMW sped into the driveway I had just left. A woman jumped out wearing spandex shorts and a T-shirt. I jogged back and introduced myself, and she invited me in for a soda.

"People around here have ZIP-code-itis," said the woman, Mimi Johnson, sipping a glass of diet Coke. "Living here is a notch in their belt. It's status. But since I was born and raised here, I don't care about that."

Johnson said she had a daughter at NYU, and I could tell in the few minutes we spoke that she was one of those cool moms, a mom you could hang out with. I also got the sense that Johnson had made out fine after her divorce but that nothing was easy these days.

"I don't like the fact that my dollar doesn't go very far here. But you adjust. You stay out of Balducci's," she said, referring to the high-end Manhattan grocery store that had recently established a Westport outpost. "Since my divorce, my income has been challenged in ways I never imagined. But I'm okay. You make it work."

Still, she said, living in a town dripping with money when you don't have as much as everybody else can be a drag, but it can also help you remember to have patience when it comes to getting and spending.

"The dollar you spend today is the dollar you don't have tomorrow. Is what you're buying a need or a want? There's a lot of haves around here. My daughter calls from NYU, where there's kids who have everything, and she'll say, 'I'm starving.' And I'm funneling out thousands every month. My father's golden rule is 'You've got to earn two or three dollars for every dollar you spend.'

He would see me buy something new when I was growing up and he'd say, 'Do you know I had to earn two hundred dollars for that hundred you just spent?' "

Johnson's work as an interior decorator (she also has a background in retail, at Saks Fifth Avenue and at her own store) gave her an insider's view of what kind of wealth, exactly, had been migrating to Westport. "People ask me, 'What can you do with ten thousand dollars?' I look at them and I say, 'That's your TV and your sofa. Maybe you shouldn't have built this huge house.' "

Johnson survives in Westport by thinking about every dollar. She had the house, she had the car, and she had a little time to regroup after her divorce, to try to figure out what direction her career should take. That advice from her father was earnest stuff, easy for a teenage girl to brush off. But now she lived it. "Sometimes I buy a little gift for myself and then *bam*—something comes along where I need *just* that amount of money. So I learned not to do that," she said. "I have a lot of friends who are one financial mistake away from disaster. What you have, you hang on to for a reason."

On the surface, Mimi Johnson appears quite lucky. A single mother with a daughter in college and a career in transition is not the person I expected to find pulling a European sports car into her driveway a few yards from the beach in upper-crust Connecticut. But she did not appear to take anything in this picture for granted; her sense of caution was real. She had earned her wisdom. I could hear the worry in the back of her throat, and I could hear the love in her voice when she spoke of her daughter, who was thudding around upstairs. It was her daughter who made Johnson remember her father's golden rule.

Keep Your Cool – It's a Big Part of Persevering

"I think it was really bad luck. But at the same time, it was good in that I went through a superhorrible experience early on."

My friend Scott Zdanis, a credit-card-processing mogul whose full story you'll read in the next chapter, started a business right out of college and today has a rented waterfront house in Miami, his own yacht, and a fleet of collectible cars. He's done well, but starting his business wasn't easy. One morning in the early days, his largest client called and said to Zdanis, essentially, "You know that thirty thousand dollars we pay you each month? No more. We're backing out of the deal."

These days, Zdanis's company's revenues *increase* an average of $30,000 a month, but back then, $30,000 was "a super, incredible, gigantic amount of money to me," he said. "It was the difference between me netting a little bit of money every month and losing a lot." Zdanis sued for breach of contract, adding the pressure and expense of a legal battle to the devastating loss of income. He won, but it was a Pyrrhic victory—the delinquent company couldn't pay him much of the settlement, and Zdanis had lost time and money chasing it. "I've got a paper that says I deserve the money. That's worth about as much as nothing," he said.

Zdanis knew that the offending company had been doing business with other high-risk companies and that the alliance was uncertain from the start. But for the relationship to come to such an abrupt halt sideswiped Zdanis's young company. The experience could have put him out of business, and many other people might have bailed. But he chose not to allow someone else's actions dictate his life. His theory is that no matter how crushing the blow, there is almost always a choice. He wanted success too badly to let this stop him. In fact, he decided he would use it to his advantage.

"I responded first in the practical way and said, 'Okay, how do we deal with this? What adjustments can we make, so we can still afford to run this business without that thirty grand a month?' At first there was some of that clear, logical thinking," he said. "My next emotion was a lot of anger and resentment. Certainly this experience demotivated me a little, and it created a tremendous amount of stress. You start really finding out who supports you and who doesn't. You start learning a lot of lessons, and maybe you also respond by saying, 'How can I protect myself better next time?' So I think that was really bad luck. But the third phase of my response was to turn it around. I realized that maybe it was good, in that I went through a superhorrible ordeal early on, and because of going through it early on, for one thing, I got myself some fantastic attorneys. And I have better, more ironclad contracts with all my processors than I would have if I'd never gone through that nightmare. So does that make it good luck? I think it does."

Zdanis alchemized the gut-punching loss of income, spinning it into a lesson that has stuck with him and helped him make boatloads of money. Even in his midtwenties, when this problem struck, that's the way he interpreted any ostensibly bad experience: as a tool to make his company stronger. Not once during the debacle did he ask himself whether he could afford to stay in business. In his mind, staying in business—somehow, some way—was a given.

Don't Deviate from Your Planned Path to Get a Quick Gain

"We were an overnight success. It just took twelve years."

Having typed *perseverance* repeatedly in this chapter, I am coming to understand the weight of that word. It implies hard work. It connotes struggle, obstacles, adversaries. When I think of someone persevering, his sleeves are rolled up, his jaw is clenched, and his brow is sweating. He's been whacked around, and he has pushed on. Perseverance makes people admire you, but it doesn't sound like much fun.

Actually, it can be.

To be able to persevere, you must be patient. As a matter of fact, patience is a hugely underrated ingredient in the building of wealth. Bob Grosnoff, the former stockbroker in Arizona (at the beginning of this chapter), sweated for years before his bond-peddling plan worked; others might have given up. But he was patient. He knew that if the outcome was what he'd hoped, his perseverance would prove worthwhile. Above all its other connotations, *perseverance* implies longevity. It means sticking to an idea with the belief that it is right — and doing so for longer than most people would.

One of the clearest, most striking examples of perseverance I have seen comes from my own life, not from knocking on someone's door. But it would be a shame not to share it here.

Among my first jobs was managing a band. I did a lot of the driving to gigs, helped with the finances, worked out logistics, and tried not to break any of the equipment. The guys in the band were three of my closest friends, and I signed on because I thought it would be fun. And it was, no question. Only later, after I had climbed out of the tour van for the last time and moved on, did I appreciate how hard those guys worked. As an independent band, they were faithful to their beliefs about music, creativity, and the way business should be conducted—even when everyone else in the music industry told them they were crazy.

The band, Dispatch, recorded its first record with borrowed money, which they later paid back. They repeated that pattern again and again until they could afford to pay for their recording and touring costs with money they'd made themselves. After six or seven years, their record sales had climbed into the hundreds of thousands—CDs sold online, in record stores, at concerts, and out of the back of the van. They were getting big. Not necessarily famous, but big enough that when they showed up in towns where they had never set foot, they found hundreds of fans singing along.

Inevitably, the music industry started paying attention, and that was exciting. The band got a lawyer. They went to meetings with executives in Manhattan skyscrapers. They played larger and larger venues, and they eventually retired the smelly blue Ford Econoline and started cruising around the country in a tour bus. (Bunk beds, a television, a driver—much better than four guys stuffed into the Econoline, sleeping sitting up, peeing into juice bottles, foraging for T-shirts off the floor when it was time to change clothes. I, of course, quit during the van era.)

Eventually, the offers came. Big offers for big record deals. But there were problems: The record companies made it clear that they would always have final say over the creative product. Plus, the companies wanted to *re*record the songs the band had already recorded and sold. To the band, this was preposterous and illogical. Record these songs again? As it was, Dispatch could barely keep up with demand for their CDs. And the only reason the music companies were even paying attention was that the band was attracting tons of fans who enjoyed the songs as recorded. Creatively, the band was at its peak. Why would they want to go back and redo what they had already done? To give the record company suits some slick, overproduced three-minute songs that would get radio play? For money? No, thanks anyway. If things kept going the way they were, the band reasoned, the money would keep coming. But profit was never the point of Dispatch. They did need income, however, at least to keep gas in the bus and to pay the crew that was now handling the increasing amount of equipment.

Dispatch passed on all the record offers. They believed that good music didn't have to be owned by people who rarely saw the faces of the fans. The three musicians, Pete Francis, Chad Stokes, and Brad Corrigan, saw their fans — their customers — every night. When they sold a CD, instead of keeping some paltry percentage of the revenue, they kept it all. They were the performers, and they were also the record company, and that's how they liked it.

That's very nice, you might be thinking, but those guys passed up millions of dollars. Well, yes, at the time they did. But a few years later, something remarkable happened. In 2004, Dispatch had mostly stopped performing, for various reasons, and they decided to formally bid their fans farewell with a free outdoor concert in Boston. Some thought 20,000 people might turn up. The morning of the show, which was scheduled to begin at five in the evening, Pete and I arrived at the site, and someone told us there were already 45,000 people there. Six hours before the show was scheduled to start. By the end, after nine o'clock at night, the Boston police had called in reinforcements for crowd control. They closed Storrow Drive, one of the city's main traffic arteries, which ran alongside the venue. I heard one cop backstage say, "Who the hell *are* these guys?" That night, on the local TV news, it was reported that the official police estimate was 110,000 people.

That's also very nice, you might be thinking, but it was *free*—of course people showed up. And the band didn't make any money. Well, a few years later, another remarkable thing happened. Somebody had the idea of a reunion show. Venues were discussed, and Madison Square Garden came up. As in the twenty-thousand-seat venue in New York City, the World's Most Famous Arena. A show was planned for a Friday night the next summer. When tickets went on sale, the show sold out in thirty minutes. So the band announced another show, on Saturday. That one sold out too, in twenty minutes. They added a third show, Sunday. Sold out.

"We were an overnight success; it just took twelve years," Francis said after the three-night set. Dispatch had been patient. Many bands, even the ones who profess not wanting to sign big corporate deals, end up doing exactly that—and hey, it's tough to blame them. It's a big business, and the money that's offered to young musicians must seem like a lottery jackpot. But by sticking to what they believed, Dispatch got its payday, bringing in more than a million dollars in ticket sales over three nights.

They gave every penny to charity.

Perseverance Doesn't Take Forever

"I'm retiring. On Tuesday! I'm only forty-seven!"

The story of Dispatch's assiduousness echoes those of others I met in my travels who made an unremitting commitment to a goal and kept their heads down until they reached it. Two of these tales are of women from Westport, Connecticut. At the end of my long day there, I stopped for a bite at Tarantino, an Italian restaurant across from the commuter rail station, where loads of Manhattan commuters spilled out of trains every hour. Aside from a meal, I was also hoping to grab one last interview — an investment banker stopping for a beer before heading home, perhaps, or maybe a successful retired couple out for dinner. I sat at the bar flipping through my notes from the day, sipping Chianti and enjoying a plate of gnocchi with veal ragu. After walking around for seven hours on a cold, windy day, I could not have imagined a more perfect meal. Soon bored with my handwriting, I let my eyes wander out the window toward the lights of the station.

In 1997, when I worked as a newspaper reporter in Westport, I wrote a series of stories under the banner "A Day in the Life." I'd find some interesting person in town and follow them around all day, chronicling their every riveting move. For the first installment, I wrote about Martha Stewart, who lived in Westport at the time and had just built a large television studio in town. Martha was the only famous person in the series; after her, I focused on regular folk, the people you see every day but know nothing about. The pieces were okay — they were conceived to give Westporters a view into their neighbors' homes and jobs and lives, the idea being that such knowledge would foment a greater sense of community. Or something like that.

As I sat at Tarantino's bar, I recalled someone who had starred in one of my favorite columns. One evening I had noticed a woman selling flowers in the parking lot of the commuter rail station. She was gregarious, cheery, and seemed to be doing a healthy business. I approached her and asked where she got the flowers, and she told me that she drove into Manhattan's flower district (who knew there was one?), on the city's West Side, each morning around four. There, in the dimness of dawn, the wholesalers rattled open the doors to their storefront garages to reveal small warehouses stocked to the ceiling with crate upon crate of flowers that had arrived at JFK or Newark just hours before—from South America, from the Middle East, from California. I accompanied the woman, whose name was Susan Valois, on one of her morning buys the following week. She moved like a Marrakechi woman at a souk, picking her way through what must have been hundreds of thousands of stems, inspecting a bloom in this crate, a bud in that one, calling out her orders to men who rushed around hugging huge bundles of daffodils and birds-of-paradise, the smoke from their cigarettes fighting with the fragrance of the flowers.

We escaped the city before eight in the morning, just as the deluge of commuters was flooding in. In Valois's garage, we clipped the thorns from roses and gathered stems into bouquets in preparation for her evening sales. She told me she had worked with some of New York City's most exclusive florists, doing parties for Elton John and Madonna. In Westport, she sold all of her flowers every night. She told me how lucky she was to have such a great job.

Yes, she's fortunate to have a job she loves. But luck? If that's what you want to call the years she spent learning the business, mastering the artistry of flowers, and waking before dawn.

Sitting at Tarantino, I looked across the street at the train station parking lot and wondered if Valois had been there earlier in the evening.

Next to me at the bar, a woman in her late forties was engrossed in the menu. She was ordering takeout. After telling the bartender her own order, she continued to stare at the menu and muttered aloud, "What should I get for him?"

"This," I said.

She looked up at me and then at my gnocchi.

"Really?"

"Really. I mean, I like it. It's delicious."

She turned to the exceedingly patient bartender. "And one of that, please. And a Pinot Grigio while I wait."

Having done her a good turn, I seized the moment and told her about my door knocking. She smiled a lot and was easy to talk to. I asked if she had a story to tell, and she kind of laughed, as if I wasn't going to believe what she was about to tell me.

"Well, I'm retiring," said the woman, whose name was Susan Anderson. "On Tuesday! I'm only forty-seven!"

She was right: I was dumbstruck by this information. Forty-seven? We both took sips of our wine, I uncapped my pen one last time that day, and she proceeded to tell me about how she had spent the past two decades saving toward a goal, and that it had worked, which seemed to amaze even her.

"In 2001, I sold my house in Westport and put everything I had into an apartment in Tribeca," the pricey neighborhood in lower Manhattan, she said. "I closed on that apartment nine days before nine-eleven. I was walking my dog when I saw the first plane hit—we had already moved in. I thought I had made the worst mistake of my life." People told her to sell, but she thought, No. She had a plan, and this was the plan. She had worked at the same talent agency for more than twenty years, had saved and saved, and she was moving into the dream apartment in the city. This was the plan.

Well?

"I just sold it, in October," she said. (This was February 2006.) "And it *tripled*. And I'm retiring. On *Tuesday!*"

In September 2001, Anderson had paid $1.2 million for her Tribeca dream apartment. Four years later, she sold it for $3.6 million.

Turns out she had done this sort of thing before—buying and selling houses at nice profits—and she had played by one simple rule: "Find the cheapest house in the coolest neighborhood." It wasn't new, and it wasn't rocket science, but it also never seemed to me like a real strategy before. Wasn't there a reason those houses were cheap?

Well, yes, but "location, location, location" isn't a cliché for nothing. And Anderson was proof that her simple trick could be pulled off—three times in a row, in fact, over a twenty-year period. She bought her first house in Westport in 1985 for $185,000 and sold it three years later for $320,000. "I bought the crappiest house in Westport. It doesn't matter—someone is going to want to live there, especially once you make it look like a Pottery Barn catalog, which you can do for cheap. There's no bigger payoff than to get it when it's disgusting," she said. With those earnings, she bought another house in town for $545,000, and she held on to it for seven years before selling it for $985,000. After that, she sprang for the Tribeca place.

What were her retirement plans, I asked? She didn't seem the type to move to Boca for shuffleboard and early-bird specials at Red Lobster.

"I'm going to produce a Broadway show," she said, barely able to get the words out through her smile. She had bought the rights to the 1951 Alec Guinness movie *The Man in the White Suit*.

"You can do this," she told me. "But it has to be in a neighborhood that's *going* to be Westport for a long time. That way you get the *bump*"—an amount of money that elevates you to early-retirement status. This belief was key to her holding on to the Tribeca place. She had faith that lower Manhattan would rebound—a faith many people did not share—and she held fast to it. "I loved working at the talent agency, and it paid a lovely salary, but it doesn't give you enough to get *out*. Even buying a place and renting it out doesn't give you the bump."

This was more than a lesson about timing the real estate market or speculating on hot neighborhoods. It was about patience and steadfastness. The higher the stakes, the easier it is to doubt yourself. And the more trying the circumstances, the more tempting it is to divert from your plan. After 9/11, Anderson wasn't the only one doubting the future. The stock market burrowed into the dirt as nervous investors pulled out. But within months, some of the hardest-hit sectors had actually rebounded to pre-9/11 levels, and some soared even higher. Anderson might have been mistaken, thinking that the value of her new home would eventually do the same. But if she had dumped it at the time, she could have been absolutely certain of only one fact: that she would lose money.

Once You Find Your Calling, Persevering Is Easy

"I guess it's just my personality.
I have this curiosity that has served me quite well."

Far away from the Connecticut shore, in another waterfront home, I met a man who had stuck with the same business for fifty-one years. Exact same thing, year after year. Wait till you hear what it was.

A college friend of mine in Lake Forest, Illinois, had recommended I visit this particular house when I was in town. "Knock on Frank's door," his parents said. "He's got a great story. He got lucky, hit it big." They didn't tell me what Frank's story was.

I had been to Lake Forest more than a decade earlier, to visit the same friend. I remember driving to the center of town for a sandwich and parking in front of a Ferrari dealership. The sandwich had aioli on it, not mayo, which at the time seemed fancy to me. In 2007, the median household income in Lake Forest was $164,906, and the average value of a home was $929,715. It ranked number thirty on my list of the hundred richest ZIP codes.

It was hard to believe that Frank Heurich's mansion once served as the garage for another house. He had obviously added on, and now his white house stood tall and broad. On the other side of an endless lawn that could accommodate multiple football games simultaneously, Lake Michigan rippled, a thin watercolor stripe above the green expanse. I sat in a chair that was like a pile of cotton balls. Heurich seemed to wonder from the outset what was so interesting about him, and I had to ask a lot of questions. He looked vaguely like Dick Cheney, without the crooked smirk, and wore a faded purple Northwestern University sweatshirt and jeans.

"I started a company called Gregor Jonsson Shrimp Peeling Systems with a guy who had a retail fish business in Highland Park," he said flatly. "We make and lease machines to peel and deliver shrimp."

I stared at him, unmoving, for probably too long a moment. I glanced outside at the huge lawn and the shimmering lake beyond. I looked back at Frank Heurich.

"Shrimp peeling?" I asked.

"Yeah."

After another moment, I said something like, "Wow." And then, "What was the other guy's name, who had the fish business?"

Heurich stared at me.

"Gregor Jonsson."

"Right," I said.

Jonsson, a family friend, was much older than Heurich. At his fish store, Jonsson and his small staff filleted the fish themselves and peeled shrimp by hand—which at the time was the only option. One day, an employee stood hunched over the shrimp table, peeling away, and muttered, "They should make a machine to do this."

It was one of those lightbulb moments. Jonsson took a paper clip, grabbed a shrimp by the swimmerets—those are the little legs—and he held it in place somehow with the paper clip, cut it down the back with scissors, then got the veins out with an ice pick. He worked for the next fourteen years on making a machine that could do the same thing.

Meanwhile, Heurich had been off getting an undergraduate business degree with a concentration in marketing from the University of Illinois ("It was cheap," he said) and an MBA from the University of Chicago. By the time Heurich finished school, Jonsson had almost perfected his shrimp-peeling machine, and he needed a business-minded partner, someone better at accounting, hiring, and generally turning a profit. He called Heurich.

The pair came up with an unusual business model: they wouldn't sell the machines, they would lease them. The company assumes 100 percent of the risk, but the machines generate income for as long as they are operational. "Gregor just thought we could make more money that way," Heurich said. "So we do a month-to-month lease." For more than fifty years now, his company has been collecting money off month-to-month leases. Other companies have tried to replicate Gregor Jonsson's product, but none have matched it. One key advantage, which no one has been able to mimic, is that Heurich's machines do not require the shrimp to be of uniform size. "There's another company that does what we do, but they squeeze the shrimp and pinch the meat out," Heurich said. "We do it totally differently. With us, size differences from shrimp to shrimp are not an issue. We can do shrimp of all different sizes. We can peel it completely or leave the tail on. We can butterfly it, whatever." All I could think of at that moment was Bubba in *Forrest Gump*. "We have patents, but our protection is mostly that it's very expensive machinery to produce. It would be difficult for someone to do what we do." (The company has a terrific short video on its Web site, www.jonsson .com, that shows how the machines work.)

I pressed Heurich about the month-to-month lease model. It fascinated me. These machines were expensive to build and maintain, and I assumed that the company could command a high price by selling them to seafood distributors and restaurants. But Heurich said that not only was the leasing model more profitable (and who was I to argue, sitting in his giant house?), customers liked it better.

"That business model makes sense for us because we have a very small, niche market, and by leasing and replacing the machines on a schedule, we can offer the best-quality products and service," he said. "When we started out, the machines were not always perfect, and by leasing them, we could afford to keep updating and improving them and replacing them with new ones. The way our leasing program works, there's no long-term obligation for the customer. We take all the risk. This has several advantages: The first is that we don't need as big a sales effort, which is expensive to have. And we don't have any of the legal expenses that you need to collect on defaults and things like that. We're a very small company, so we need to operate efficiently. By assuming all the risk, we're announcing that we have confidence in our product and that we can keep the customer happy."

After a moment, he added, "Usually it works out. It doesn't always work out. But that's the nature of risk. And what's risk? What's the worst that could happen? I'll still be alive."

Growing up, Heurich learned about customer service by working in his father's jewelry store. There he learned that for a small business, serving people is more important than any other task—research, development, accounting, hiring, marketing, anything.

"I started working for my father when I was about twelve. That experience—taking care of customers—made me realize where the money comes from. It comes from the customers! That was very valuable for me," he said. Heurich also had an aptitude for working with his hands, which he improved by repairing clocks and jewelry clasps. He enjoyed learning about engineering and mechanics. So, he had an interest in accounting and he liked working with his hands—these became the foundation for his career running a business that makes machines, he said, and once he found a job that combined his loves, he stuck to it.

"I guess it's just my personality. I have this curiosity that has served me quite well, I think. Some people want to know about one small area. They want to be specialists. But I have curiosity in other areas. I want to know about all areas of the business," he said.

Heurich was a model of resoluteness, but I wondered if he enjoyed his work—particularly after doing the same thing for so many years. When I asked him if he ever thought about branching out or adding new machines to the product line, if even just to bust up the routine, he said, in the pleasant, matter-of-fact way that midwesterners state what seems obvious to them, "We haven't expanded very far because we felt there would always be opportunity in our business. Shrimp is a huge market. So we stayed in the area of what we thought we knew best. We do have a new product we're bringing out soon, which is for working with cold-water shrimp." He paused for a moment before shrugging and adding, "But it's still shrimp."

In the next chapter, you'll read about people who fell in love with their work to the point of obsession: Dave Dollinger, a Silicon Valley real estate mogul who lives for the thrill of the deal; Rena Holman, a charming art dealer I met in Palm Beach, who loves to match people with works of art; and a woman in Austin who felt inspired to be one of the first employees of Dell Computer Corporation, working until all hours, excited by the uncertainty of the future. They cherished their jobs. Did Heurich, I asked?

"I have four kids, and all of them and their spouses are working for me. Seven out of the twenty employees are family," he said. "We're doing very well—we just moved to a new facility that's twice as big as our old space, where we had been for forty-five years. And this company suits my personality. I love food, I have mechanical aptitude, I have business and selling aptitude. And I love shrimp. It's low in fat, it's healthy, it can't live in polluted waters. I love it. As long as it's not overcooked."

Frank Heurich has plugged away, running his business the best way he knows how, for more than five decades. I'm sure Gregor Jonsson, Inc., Shrimp Peeling Systems has taken its share of hits over the years—disappointing quarters, manufacturing glitches, client disputes, that kind of thing—but listening to Heurich, you come away with the impression that his steward-ship has kept the company running about as smoothly as a small business can. He is pleased to be able to use both his MBA and his hands, and that's all the satisfaction he needs. He hasn't tried to take off in pursuit of dramatic growth at the expense of maintaining his core business—didn't try to invent an oyster-shucking machine or an automatic lobster desheller—and in re-maining steadfast, he has achieved the long, slow, steady ascension to—well, to the mansion on Lake Michigan in ZIP code number thirty.

Remember That You Can't Do a Business Transaction with Yourself

"That's one of the biggest secrets to a successful business life, I think: paying the people you owe money to."

About two thousand miles west of Frank Heurich's house, Edith Caldwell's home floats in the waters of San Francisco Bay. Caldwell lives in a houseboat docked in a picturesque marina across the street from a row of storefronts. One of those shops houses the Edith Caldwell Gallery, where she sells fine paintings, cotton tap-estries, and objets d'art.

Caldwell is one of my out-of-bounds stories, someone I met not by randomly knocking on doors but by other means, as I made my way around the country. When I traveled to San Fran-cisco to ring doorbells in Silicon Valley, my wife, then a few months pregnant with our first child, flew out to meet me for a long weekend. She had a grand time seeing the Museum of Mod-

ern Art and perusing North Beach in San Francisco while I
knocked and rang a few miles south, in Atherton. One afternoon,
she and I drove over the Golden Gate Bridge to the Marin Head-
lands, where we trekked out to the Point Bonita Lighthouse. We
stopped for dinner in Sausalito and happened upon Caldwell's
cozy gallery. I was in information-gathering mode, and I couldn't
help but ask the proprietor, a slender, elegant woman with cropped,
snowy hair and wearing a navy blue suit and pearls, if she had any
wisdom to share.

One of the first things she said to me was: "My main focus is
to show people the wonderful things that man can do rather than
the horrible things he can do." As mission statements go, it
sounded worthwhile.

Caldwell seemed like one of those lucky people we encounter
every so often and wonder why the heavens sprinkled magic dust
on them and not us—why *they* get to have perfect lives. Caldwell
had run her gallery for many years, most as a single mother raising two children, who were eighteen and twenty at the time we
met. She said she had made some smart real estate investments in
the early 1990s, which certainly didn't hurt the college fund. But
to sustain her business over so many years, she had developed a
couple of business habits that showed real wisdom.

First, she pays her artists their cut as soon as she sells a work.
Even if she needs the money at that moment to pay another bill,
she pays the artist first. It's the only way to avoid bad debts, she
said, which can bring down a business. This tenet, of course, applies to more than the art world. In fact, it echoes a general attitude that everyone featured in this chapter shares: Don't mess
with the plan for the wrong reasons. Don't wander from the core
mission for the sake of convenience. "Everyone should remember

that, whether you run a store or you're a contractor—anyone who has suppliers to pay. That's one of the biggest secrets to a successful business life, I think: paying the people you owe money to with the money that is supposed to go to them. And if you can't, then call them and tell them the situation. Even if you're going to lose a sale. You have to be honest," she said.

Second, she always remembers her purpose, why she works so hard at knowing her industry and running her business well. "I look at my job as enabling people to get what they want. There was a couple in here today. They were from Ireland, and they bought a tapestry. They really wanted it, but they couldn't figure out how they were going to pay for it. I said, 'You can take as long as you want to pay for it. And I don't charge any interest.' They asked me how much they would have to leave as a deposit, and I said, 'As much as you're comfortable with.' Now, I won't ship it to them until they pay for it—that tends to speed things up—but I wanted to help them get it."

Caldwell likes to say that by selling art, she is helping to spread beauty: "I don't try to anticipate what people will buy. I try to sell what I think will be worthy of putting out on the planet. I think these things make the world a better place." In other words, she considers her customers and her suppliers to be of equal importance. By respecting and watching out for the artists whose work she sells and the customers who buy it, she virtually assures herself repeat business on both sides.

The result has been a long, steady upward climb for the Edith Caldwell Gallery. "I love being here on the first floor because I get to see all these jillion people, and they get to come in and see this art," she said. "People get detached from reality in the best way." A move from downtown San Francisco to idyllic Sausalito helped the bottom line too, even though it meant decamping from the city center and setting up shop in a tourist town. "Eighty percent of my business comes from tourists. A tourist who buys a piece of art becomes an out-of-town client. The location is perfect. A lot of clients are couples who are together on vacation. They tell me they never wander around looking for art at home."

I asked her if, as a single mother running a small business, she experienced many days when the pressures of parenthood on top of entrepreneurship seemed too much to bear.

"What? No," Caldwell said, shaking her head. "No! See, it's a really easy job. My hours are eleven to five. I had children, so those were the perfect hours. But the thing is, I have made the money that I needed to make. I don't do it to see how much money I can make. I do it to support myself and the children. And that enables me to go to work at eleven o'clock in the morning."

Prepare to Get Lucky

"It's not just how much you put in, it's how soon you put it in."

I was thinking about my father as I sat at the rustic wood table in Dave and Ruth Frederickson's kitchen in Paradise Valley, Arizona. Dave was seventy-three and had owned and run a heavy equipment distributorship. He was tall and thin, with gray straw hair, and he wore a bright white shirt and pressed khakis. As we spoke, two dachshunds scampered around our feet, barking. Outside, mountains shadowed the Fredericksons' oval swimming pool.

"Any bonus or extra money I ever got, half went to debt or savings, and half went to play—vacations and things. That philosophy has worked out pretty well for us," Dave said. He was a practical man, I could tell, even on the subject of leisure. He understood its importance, but he said he also thought a lot about the future at all times. "You've *got* to be aware of how much money it takes to retire. Don't wait until you're sixty-two to put money aside, and don't expect an inheritance. Nowadays, your parents might live until they're ninety! My view of personal finance is that it's a three-legged stool: Social Security, personal savings, and a company retirement plan—a 401(k) or a pension. The idea is to get as much money in as you can early on. It's not just how much you put in, it's how soon you put it in. It's being aware. When you get to your forties and fifties, if you want to have a standard of living, you've got to plan ahead."

The Fredericksons had four children, and they took them camping, skiing in Arizona and Colorado, boating on Lake Powell. Ruth, an elegant woman with a cloud of white hair, had stayed home to raise the children. Family was important, and the couple's attention to their kids had yielded one particularly sweet dividend: all four—plus grandchildren—live in the Phoenix area. A picture from a recent family reunion hung on the wall. There were enough people to stage a barn raising.

Like my own parents, Dave and Ruth had wrung the most possible enjoyment out of the money Dave earned while also playing it safe. Early in his career, Dave had invested aggressively, slowly changing his strategy toward the end. "When you're young, don't just put it in a money market fund. Of course, these days our retirement money is parked in stable principals. I retired at sixty-eight, so when I was sixty-three or so, I shifted away from anything that was growth," he said, nodding his head.

"Too many people live for today and think they'll be taken care of," Ruth added, shaking her head. "I have one friend who's eighty-two and still working."

"We've been in this house for sixteen years," Dave said, nodding. "We'll make a lot of money on it. You go to bed at night feeling good."

"Our kids won't have to take care of us," said Ruth.

I asked the couple, who may be two of the most pleasant people I've met, if they had ever been derailed by an occasional surprise along the steady path they had stayed on, if their patience had ever been tried or their resolve shaken. Dave thought for a minute and said, "Well, I was counting on the stock market at one point. But we've had very little growth in the portfolio. You can't just count on an eight percent return compounded."

They both nodded, solemnly.

What I learned from the people in this chapter is that lucky people are patient, or maybe it's the other way around: patient people get lucky. The kind of person we think of as lucky probably plugged away for years with a big, sometimes vague goal—and a belief that all of this will pay off in the long run. The hard work, the sweat, the nervous stomachaches, the anxiety, the perseverance—you have to believe it's going to count. That's a hard thing to do. Bob Grosnoff, the dauntless stockbroker at the beginning of the chapter, watched his colleagues make a quick buck while he toiled for bigger riches that he hoped would come later. And the indefatigable members of Dispatch, the most successful independent band you've probably never heard of, sometimes had to grit their teeth as they passed up big-time record deals, reassuring themselves that it was the right decision. Edith Caldwell stuck to basic tenets of business practice that she firmly believed in, allowing her to succeed, as a single woman, in an unpredictable field.

Patience, by nature, requires faith. If you don't have faith that your tenacity will pay off—that it will lead you to a lucky day— chances are it won't. And with faith, sometimes, comes passion, and even a healthy brand of obsession. That's what the next chapter is about.

THREE

THE ECONOMICS OF OBSESSION

You Need More Than Passion – You Need an Intensity That Will Scare People

Are some people born with more drive than others? Sometimes it appears that way. My mother told me a story recently about my older brother, Michael. When I was six and he was seven, our family moved to a bigger house up the street from the cozy one (six people, 1,400 square feet) where he and I had learned to walk and talk and tie our shoes and shoot a basketball. Mike and I had always shared a room with bunk beds, but now we had our own rooms. The sense of autonomy was thrilling, and we quickly established our own independent territories at either end of the short upstairs hall.

One night a few weeks after the family had settled in, with unpacked boxes still stacked in corners and framed pictures leaning against walls where they were to be hung, my mother walked down the hall to Mike's small room, which faced the backyard. He should have been asleep, but she found the shades up and him lying in bed, staring at the moon, sheets bunched at his feet. She asked if everything was okay.

"I just get so excited about all the things I want to invent that I start kicking my feet and I can't stop," he said.

When I picture Mike's room in that house, I see stacks of *Popular Mechanics* magazines, the pages folded over and marked with notes; a tabletop drafting board and a T square, a sheet of graph paper taped carefully on the surface, bearing the beginnings of a sketch for a tank or a tree fort; and, everywhere, the tools a boy requires to dream up the ideas that keep him up at night: pads of tracing paper, mugs full of mechanical pencils, jars of rubber cement, X-acto knives, Scotch tape, spiral notebooks.

Maybe Mike was born with more creativity and ambition than the other kids on our block—after all, none of them built a two-story tree house with an elevator and windows and a zip wire connecting it to the opposite end of the yard. But there are two other possible explanations for why our backyard boasted the biggest and most enjoyable eyesore in the neighborhood: Perhaps the other kids were pouring themselves into different interests, like puppetry or long division or playing the cello, and perhaps their proficiency in these areas was world class, just like Mike's tree house–building acumen. Or, maybe, because Mike (and I and our two sisters) grew up in a household that encouraged creativity and hard work, he discovered talents and interests that may have remained dormant if he had grown up in, say, a coal-mining family in northern Russia. (I'm not 100 percent certain that people mine coal in northern Russia, but if they do, I bet there's not a lot of time spent sketching late at night and building tree houses.)

Either way, my brother was obsessed with invention. Not interested, not curious, not even merely passionate—obsessed. He couldn't sleep because his feet kicked uncontrollably with excitement. He spent hours in the tree, hammering, sawing, scheming, sweating. He focused his energy on an achingly specific dream, and he spent every free minute making it come true. Later in life, he channeled his obsession into becoming an investment banker on Wall Street, specializing in something I don't quite understand. He still stays up late and, his wife recently told me, still gets what she has termed "waggy feet."

A lot of people tell you that you have to be passionate about your work. You have to love what you do. Only then will you find real happiness and reward.

Well, of course. The obviousness of that advice makes my eyes roll. These people haven't completed the puzzle. I have come to see passion and obsession as two degrees of dedication that are quite different. When it comes to your vocation, passion is simply love for your work—the feelings of fulfillment and happiness that your work brings you. Wonderful thing, passion. Obsession, though, is the single-minded, even maniacal pursuit of a goal. Obsession comes when passion blooms, fertilized with hard work, cleverness, shrewdness, and everything else that makes a person want to follow a dream. Obsession is the fun part.

None of the people I met when I traveled the country—not a single one, as I scan the list—appears to have been born with some special gene for success. If you want to be three inches taller, that's too bad. But if you possess an obsessive desire to be happier in your career and to feel more excited about the future, you've got far better odds, judging from the stories people told me.

Find a Driver Other Than Money – It's Usually More Lucrative Than Money Alone

"If you find something you love, and it's in a field where there's money to be made, you will make it. But that – the money – can't be why *you go into that field in the first place."*

The first door I knocked on in Sandy Springs, Georgia, was hinged to what, for all the world, looked like an Italian villa. Sandy Springs happened to be the last town I visited over the course of the year I spent researching this book, and I had seen plenty of overdone Italian-style mansions in squeaky subdivisions: faux pillars, trompe l'oeil cypress trees painted on walls, plaster naked-cherub fountains spluttering in the center islands of circular driveways. This particular house, shining bright on a high corner lot that bubbled above the rest of the street's leafy topography, was different. I've been to Italy, and here it was, twenty minutes outside of Atlanta.

As I had discovered in a few other states, if you drive fifteen minutes *past* the suburb everyone knows is full of rich people, you often find the real money. The one-acre lots become two- and three-acre lots, there are fewer shops downtown — shops attract people, and people play music loud and drive too fast — and the on-street parking restrictions tighten. This is true of lovely burghs like Gates Mills, Ohio, one town past old-money Shaker Heights; Paradise Valley, Arizona, on the outskirts of Scottsdale; and Sandy Springs, which became an official town only recently (it used to be part of Atlanta proper), just past wealthy, but crowded, Buckhead.

Many of the houses I saw in Sandy Springs fell into one of two categories: There were gargantuan, four-car-garage McMansions whose fresh-from-the-nursery landscaping hadn't grown in yet—dwarfish, clipped bushes poking through pungent mulch in the shadow of soaring facades. And then there were older split-levels and ranches, most of which were probably built in the middle of the twentieth century. A betting man might wager that the same families had lived in these older places for two generations. Still, the buildings and grounds were invariably kempt and well pruned—the owners obviously took pride in their humble homes, even in the face of the towering new ones that bore down on them from either side. The older homes reminded me of stalwart company men: their value was a little inflated, but their service was long and loyal despite the obvious fact that new blood would soon replace them, as it had the old men in the offices to the left and right.

I covered about six miles in Sandy Springs, all on foot, and along the way I observed a fascinating economic indicator that I feel confident in claiming to have discovered: the Construction Litter Index (CLI). On the side of nearly every street, I saw, enmeshed in crabgrass or lodged in sewer grates, the detritus of progress: a length of frayed electrical wire, its copper innards protruding from white plastic casing; tufts of pink insulation; a paint scraper that had been run over a few times; drywall screws strewn in patterns, like pick-up sticks. These are the scraps that fly off contractors' vans in neighborhoods where business is good. The more construction litter I saw, the more obvious it was that residents and developers were spending a lot of money to build, add on, and spruce up. In Sandy Springs, on a high-medium-low scale, the CLI was high.

• • •

The exterior of the Italian villa was painted the color of runny egg yolk, and it had tall, skinny windows with weathered shutters in the same dark green you see in Tuscany. The temperature in Atlanta that day hovered around ninety degrees, and I paced myself as I climbed the escarpment between the street and the house.

The house had two front doors. One was on ground level, and there was a brown UPS box leaning against it. An orphaned package on the front stoop was never a good sign for me, because it usually meant no one was home. I knocked anyway. Nothing. I was about to turn away—maybe the prospect of someone being home at the first stop of the day, and a villa no less, was too much to wish for. But on either side of the door, exterior stairs led up to another entrance directly above the first. I chose the stairs on the right.

The top door was actually two large wooden doors, thick as Oxford's unabridged. A FedEx envelope was propped against them. Another bad sign. But about forty-five seconds after I rang the bell, an eternity when you're standing on a stranger's stoop, a tiny, eye-level door built into one of the large doors opened, and a man peered out at me. It reminded me of the entrance to the castle in Oz, when the guard peeks out before letting Dorothy and her friends inside. I did not mention this to the man.

He waited for me to speak, and I told him what I was up to. Without a word, the little door closed, and a few seconds later the big door opened and he stepped outside. My opening monologue competed for his attention with the FedEx envelope, the contents of which appeared to momentarily worry or perplex him. He looked to be in his fifties, wore shorts and a blue polo shirt, and bore a passing resemblance to the writer Calvin Trillin. He invited me inside.

It became obvious within a few minutes that the owners were

the obsessive type, in the best way. The house turned out to be an exact replica, inside and out, of a sixteenth-century building called Villa Cetinale in Sovicille, Italy, near Siena. The man I was talking to, whose name was Art Dwyer, told me that the house was really his wife's baby. We went inside, and he called her in from the back patio, where she was chatting with a worker who was scrubbing a fountain that emptied into a rectangular swimming pool. Her name was Toni, and she wore a white terry-cloth robe bearing the logo of the National Hotel in Miami Beach. Dwyer gave me something called an Aquapod, a tiny, round bottle of Deer Park water, and we sat in the living room as the Discovery Channel played volumeless on a television mounted high in a corner.

Dwyer spoke authoritatively, with a heavy Boston accent, about the secrets of happy working and happy living. It was as if he had been preparing for my questions all morning—he often paused for a moment before answering, then began by saying something like, "There are two ways to do that," or "There are three reasons for that. Number one . . ." How he mentally mapped out his replies so quickly I don't know. I began by asking him how he and Toni had come to be able to build their dream house.

"First of all, to work hard to achieve the goal of just being able to afford stuff is a terrible way to go through life," he said. "If you go through med school to become a wealthy doctor, but you don't love medicine . . ." His voice trailed off and he made a face as if he had just smelled spoiled meat. After finding work you love, to elevate yourself to the highest level of success, you need a higher goal—a goal that may or may not be related to the work itself. For the Dwyers, it was this epic house that surrounded us that drove them. Not in a raw, materialistic way. They didn't covet a house like this for its own sake. They dreamed of it in their hearts, which is quite different.

Like many of the people I met around the country, Art Dwyer had begun his career in the corporate world, then quit to run his own business, which he built into a very profitable enterprise. He is in media planning, the buying and selling of advertising. In 1972, he began working at Communication Trends, a media buying and planning agency, which he and Toni bought out in the 1980s. Dwyer is now the president and chief operating officer.

"Before that, when I first started out, I was working at a very large corporation. I could have stayed there for forty years and gotten the gold watch and the whole bit," he told me. But in order to rise to the heights of a given profession, he said, you have to at least give yourself the opportunity to be the person in charge. He didn't want to disclose the name of the corporation he worked for, but he implied that it was so big that he would probably have never had the opportunity, or the desire, to become its CEO. (Although he had climbed high enough in the hierarchy that he routinely played golf with the man who *would* eventually become CEO.)

"It's a matter of finding something you love, that you're very good at. If your dream is to be successful, then get into an area where you can be the top dog in that company. Chances are if you're an accountant and you work in a hospital or an advertising agency, you're never going to run that hospital or that ad agency. You want to get into an environment where you're not saddled with doing one single task," he said.

Dwyer earned a pair of degrees that suggest an interest in mixing the curious, creative mind of an artist with the relentless forge-ahead mentality of a business executive: a journalism degree from the University of Missouri and an MBA from Drake University. He settled on business, but after working in the corporate world he knew that he wanted—or perhaps needed—to work with artistic people. "When I first went to work at the corporation, I met this two-fisted Irishman who had been a World War Two pilot and the whole thing," Dwyer said. "He asked me what I wanted to do with my life. Then he told me that the more important thing was to identify the things I *didn't* want to do." What Dwyer didn't want was pretty simple: he didn't want to work for a company that wasn't his, spend his days at a place he didn't control, and do work that he didn't love with people he had no feelings for. He knew he could make more money and have more security on his own, plus he could tailor his work—and his staff—to his liking.

He had met some of the people at Communication Trends while he still worked at the corporation, and he liked and respected them as businesspeople and as friends. Plus, now he gets to work directly with entertainment companies, including HBO, Turner Broadcasting, and Univision. He genuinely enjoys the people he works with, and that only makes him love his work more.

We all want that—work that speaks to our souls, colleagues who enlighten us and whom we enjoy. The difference is that Dwyer, like so many of the people who opened expensive, pressure-treated, golden-knockered doors to speak with me, gave it a shot. Not only that, but he left a good job at a Fortune 100 company to do it. That took guts. And intelligence, of course. Maybe he was born with more of these qualities than other people. Or maybe, like my brother Mike, he was encouraged and taught as a boy to pursue what genuinely interested him rather than settle for what most people would consider a safe job.

As Communication Trends grew, the Dwyers were cultivating a love for all things Italian. They made their first trip to Italy together in the late 1990s, when their daughter was attending school in Florence (Toni had been before, on her own). Over the years, traveling to Tuscany became something of a hobby, and they fell in love with Tuscan architecture. Toni dreamed of re-creating Villa Cetinale for about ten years before the Dwyers broke ground. With an obsession on which to focus—the house—the Dwyers concentrated on their passion: their work.

What genuinely interested them was the creative business of advertising. They loved it, and this drove them to work hard at networking and pleasing clients. But they also had the ambitious goal of building a villa in suburban Georgia, so they focused on growing their business to a size they otherwise might not have reached for.

I reminded them that lots of people go into advertising, and lots of people love it and work hard at it, and lots of people even run their own firms. But lots of people don't live in mansions in the seventy-seventh richest ZIP code in the United States of America.

"There are two ways to get there. The first is to become so good at what you do that everyone wants to buy your services," Art said. He made sure to point out that you don't have to be born good at what you do—you learn. "The second is to publicize and promote the hell out of yourself so that everyone thinks and knows you're the best. People who are very, very good at what they do but don't promote themselves make it that much more difficult for people to find them. Of course, going back to number one, it's tough to be the best at something and not get discovered by people who want what you offer."

Dwyer's point about self-promotion made me think of an informal survey administered by Carol Dweck, the Stanford University researcher I introduced in chapter 1. In the survey, which she describes in her book *Mindset,* she asked people to picture in their minds a detailed image of Thomas Edison at work. Most respondents said they imagined Edison working alone, a reclusive inventor toiling away in a darkened room while the world eagerly awaited his next invention. In fact, Dweck writes, citing Edison's biographer Paul Israel, Edison was a gifted inventor but was also a genius at self-promotion. He worked with large teams of assistants in pristine, advanced laboratories, and he knew how to make sure he was cited in the press—and went down in history—as the sole inventor of a few creations for which he might otherwise have shared the credit.

Both Dwyer and his wife were the first in their families to attend college. Their grandparents were immigrants from Italy and Ireland, and their fathers worked blue-collar jobs. "I saw my father wake up at four o'clock every morning to go to work as a door-to-door milkman for the HP Hood dairy company. I saw my mother go to a job after the kids went to school. Toni's father worked in the steel mills. So it wasn't 'Go become a doctor or a lawyer.' It was 'There are better ways to live than this. Just don't make the Rolls Royce your *goal.*' Both our families stressed education. Not so we could buy a big house or a big car; they stressed it as a way to get a better life. Our parents wouldn't live this way"—he waved a hand at the grandiosity of the room we were sitting in, the collection of antlers mounted above the fireplace, the open kitchen with copper pots hanging above an island—"even if they won the lottery. But because they stressed education, we said that if we ever get some money, we want to be able to relish those efforts. We both drive eight- to ten-year-old cars. We have no yachts, no second homes. *This* is the by-product of our efforts."

The house, he meant. And it was truly spectacular. The exposed beams in the ceiling had been collected from Italian farmhouses; the weathered floorboards were antique American chestnut. The furniture was from Italy too, and some of it dated from the sixteenth and seventeenth centuries. The vaulted ceiling in the foyer, the Italian-made hardware holding the shutters in place outside, the riveted copper top of the kitchen island — every detail, they explained, was evidence of Toni's passion for her Italian ancestry and her obsession with re-creating a monument to that heritage.

"You have to love and be committed to whatever it is you're going to spend your money on," Dwyer said. "To go out and buy a yacht because the guy next door has a yacht — that's bad." He was explaining that the house, attention grabbing and oversized though it may be, was not a vehicle for the Dwyers to advertise their wealth. It was simply what brought them pleasure, the way classic cars or squirreling away money for future generations bring other people pleasure.

"This house is a pain in the ass," Dwyer said, his eyes widening. "But the question is, What do you want to do with your money? The house is a microcosm of what we're talking about." He was using the edifice as a metaphor for his and Toni's approach to earning: just as doing work you love increases your odds of making money, building a house with such care, love, and precision increases the chances that it will become more valuable over time. He continued: "Toni was absolutely determined to make the details of the house correct. Everyone tried to talk her out of it. But now, four or five architects in the area have attempted to copy it. The value has gone way, way up. Now, that's not why we *did* it. It's just that if you do something you absolutely love, the financial rewards are more likely to happen and to last a long time. Just like with our business: if you find something you love, and it's in a field where there's money to be made, you will make it. But that—the money—can't be *why* you go into that field in the first place."

Do One Thing and Do It Well

....

"The secret of my success was that my husband was a wonderful pilot and flew for Delta Air Lines for thirty years."

....

What Art Dwyer said about combining genuine skill with marketing and self-promotion—as Thomas Edison did—is true, but there's a third ingredient that makes it easier to sell your services for high dollars: always performing at the height of your ability.

In Sandy Springs, Georgia, I met Helen Layton, a woman whose husband, Roy, had passed away many years before. She was my final interview. Nineteen ZIP codes, eleven states, fifty interviews, and then . . . Helen, eighty-two years old, standing, hands on hips, in the dogwood shade, halfway down the slope of her driveway, supervising her grown daughter, Tissy, who was planting an oak-leaf hydrangea in the dirt. When I stepped off the sidewalk and down the drive, wearing a white shirt and khakis, the two women eyed me with unmasked suspicion. Maybe even contempt. I gave them my warmest smile and told them who I was and what I was doing.

A silence hung in the thick, woolen Atlanta heat as they

looked me over, Helen folding her arms, Tissy mopping her brow.

"You're not from the water company?" Helen asked.

"I'm not from the water company," I said.

"We thought you were the man from the water company," said Tissy.

"No, ma'am."

"Oh. There's a drought on, and we had our hose on earlier. They come around and check."

Once it was established that I was not the least bit concerned about whether they irrigated their grass or not, they went back to their work. In the tone that some southern women have mastered, a distinctive mix of pride and didacticism, Layton told me that she had regularly mowed her own lawn until five years ago, when she was seventy-seven. Looking at the smooth aprons of manicured grass around the pop-up mansions that surrounded Layton's twenty-nine-year-old split-level, I wouldn't be surprised if this little old lady was the only person on the street who did her own yard work anymore. The rest of the neighborhood looked as if it had been landscaped with Astroturf and plastic shrubs. Her home was no less stately and far more elegant. The house was big, and the property was magnificent, with a small, sloping forest of trees trailing behind the house like an army.

Tissy, meanwhile, was engaged in a rather heroic bush-planting project. The hole was dug, the wheelbarrow was full of topsoil, the bush itself was trimmed and ready, and Tissy wheeled and shoveled and watered and fertilized. What made it heroic was that Tissy had only one full arm, the other a short nub. I awkwardly offered to help move the wheelbarrow or to shovel some dirt, but she cheerfully declined and continued expertly planting the bush.

Helen Layton was born in a poor speck of a town called Ty Ty, in southern Georgia (population 716 in 2000), the grand-daughter of the local constable. "He had no car. He had no *gun,* even," she said. She was now leading me into the backyard—she wanted to show me the blossoming stalks of mature hydrangeas that formed the border to the patio. I worried about her eighty-two-year-old ankles on the uneven stone steps that led around back, but she descended them like a young girl of sixty. She wore a pink blouse, pink moccasins, hot pink polish on her fingernails, and a flowing denim skirt. A pink silk-rose barrette held her pew-ter hair in a bun. She exuded small townness—she was elegant, funny, polite, and unflappable.

"My grandfather would arrest somebody and lock him up in the one jail cell, and my grandmother would bring the prisoner breakfast," she said. "My father worked as a mechanic at a filling station, and my mother had a general store. There was only one other store in town that sold groceries, Mr. Swain's. If my mom wouldn't let me have any bananas or something, I'd go over to Mr. Swain's store and put some on credit. I don't know who I thought was going to pay for it."

Sandy Springs was a long way from Ty Ty, and I asked Layton how she ended up here. "The secret of my success was that my husband was a wonderful pilot who flew for Delta Air Lines for thirty years," she said.

From the time he was a young boy, Roy Layton wanted to fly planes. Back then, families who had automobiles used to take Sunday drives, and Roy always asked his parents to drive out to a nearby airport to watch the planes. After serving as a pilot in World War II, Roy went to work in an air-traffic control tower for the Civil Aeronautics Administration, a government outfit created by Franklin Roosevelt that predated the Federal Aviation

Agency. One day, around 1950, he got a call from an Air Force buddy he knew during the war. The buddy had gone on to work for Delta Air Lines, which was headquartered in Atlanta, and had become its chief pilot. Over the phone, the pal wondered vociferously why Roy was working some crummy government job when he could be making serious money as a commercial pilot. So, in 1951, the Layton family moved to Sandy Springs, and Roy flew for Delta until 1980. "I still have a Delta pass," Helen said. "I can fly anywhere they fly. I just went down to Melbourne, Florida, three weeks ago."

We can assume that the Delta chief knew dozens of pilots from his Air Force days, and that Roy Layton probably wasn't the only one he called. But, naturally, he didn't call them all. He needed the best, and Roy's obsession with perfection — you can't be a standout pilot, military or commercial, unless you *are* obsessed with perfection — made him the ideal candidate. Layton had performed well because he had committed himself to becoming a top pilot, whether anyone was watching or not. "He just loved to fly," Helen said. "He always told stories about flying. All pilots do, and he was a pilot his whole life."

I thanked Helen Layton for talking to me and said I would let her get on with her afternoon.

"That's okay," she said, standing rod-straight on her patio, hands comfortably on her hips. "I've had a good life. Three children. It's nice telling someone about it."

Hearing about Roy Layton made me think of Frank Heurich, the shrimp-peeling magnate I wrote about in chapter 2. Both men found a niche, and their minds never wandered again. In Heurich's case, the shrimp business gave him a good living, many of his family members ended up working for him, and he enjoyed eating shrimp — a perfect situation. Judging from Helen Layton's air of contentment, she and her husband had enjoyed a similar long, steady run. The only difference was that while Heurich's career required patience, expertise, and business acumen, Layton's work demanded other skills and an obsession with his work. His was perhaps the purest, simplest story of obsession I heard anywhere.

Obsess Over Whatever Job You Have

"Having already lost a job, I knew that opportunity doesn't last forever and I'd better take advantage of it."

I worried a lot, on these trips I took, about getting busted. Not that I was doing anything illegal, but in some of the smaller towns, one phone call from a worried soccer mom, and a patrol car would have been dispatched faster than I could say "How'd you get to be so rich?" The cop couldn't have arrested me—or could he? (Was I trespassing? Harassing people? Proselytizing? Is proselytizing illegal?)—but he could have made my project very difficult by telling me to . . . well, you know, stop.

So, sometimes I called ahead. I'd call the town hall, the police department—anyplace I could alert someone in power of my impending invasion, provide the license plate number of the car I'd be driving, and generally try to vaccinate myself against calls from concerned citizens. That way, if any of my eventual targets expressed concern about the possibility of my trying to steal the silver, I could tell them not to worry because I'd spoken with Officer Friendly and everything was cool. (Once, in Westport, Connecticut, a particularly helpful police lieutenant took an interest in my project and drew me a map to the streets with the most pelf.)

Atherton, California, was one place I decided to call in advance. It's a small town, and it also happened to be the number one ZIP code on my list. The wealthiest ZIP code in the United States of America. Median household income: $226,414. Average home value: $1,236,572. Average net worth: $1,505,508. Median disposable income: $156,551. Et cetera. This one was a must.

On the town's Web site I found the name and telephone number of the mayor, one Charles Marsala. I dialed.

"Hello?"

I asked for the mayor's office.

"This is Charles."

Huh. Guy answers his own phone. Either Atherton had suddenly fallen on hard times, or the town was so freakishly rich that it eschewed a bureaucratic institution as down-market as a town hall, instead asking a warm body to slap his name on the Web site and occasionally answer the phone.

In fact, Atherton has an active populace, regular elections, a town hall, a police force, and all the rest. Probably even a dog-catcher. But governing the town from day to day apparently does not require a full-time leader, so Marsala was serving a four-year term on the town council, and, per Atherton regulation, it was his turn to be mayor for a year. He was not paid for any of this.

"Great idea," he said when I described Project Door Knock, but town laws strictly prohibited solicitation. Even though I wouldn't be selling anything, he was worried that someone would call the cops within the first three doors I tried, and, after traveling three thousand miles, I would be asked to quit after ten minutes.

Fortunately, Marsala seemed excited about my project. We brainstormed a little, and after a few minutes he made me an offer I couldn't refuse: Mayor Marsala would personally solicit interviews from some of Atherton's wealthiest residents (which is like looking for the five stripiest zebras in Africa) who also had the most interesting backstories. He even offered to set up appointments and drive me from house to house and office to office on the day of my visit.

I accepted and thanked him profusely, even though this arrangement would obliterate the randomness of going door-to-door. *But,* I thought, *should I pass up the richest town in America on a technicality?* No. A day of scheduled interviews was better than no interviews at all. Plus, riding around in Marsala's car would keep a few miles off the old shoes.

You could drive clear through America's richest ZIP code without even knowing you were there. I drove down from San Francisco after a morning rain, entering the town on an unremarkable divided highway. Later, Marsala would show me streets lined with overt opulence — palaces right up there with Versailles, behind gates like Gargamel's, flowers everywhere. Barry Bonds's former house was particularly impressive and more elegant than I might have guessed. But at first, the money seemed to be hiding.

Mayor Marsala lived in a tidy one-story house with an automatic gate at either end of the circular drive. When I arrived, a handwritten note on the door directed me to meet him in his office, which was in a small outbuilding in the back. Behind the house, a giant chessboard — so big that humans could be the pawns, rooks, knights, kings, and queens — occupied a section of the lawn. Cool.

The mayor, who had dark hair and a young face — I guessed

he was in his forties—had quite a success story of his own. He had been an entrepreneur, and like many of the self-made business-people I met around the country, he had tried one thing, hit a wall, then tried another, then another. At Tulane, he studied oil drilling and engineering. He got a great job with an oil-field ser-vice company, which helped large clients such as Exxon drill faster and better. "But then oil went from forty dollars a barrel to fif-teen, and I lost my job six months later," Marsala told me. After answering an ad in the newspaper, he took a job in sales for a Los Angeles industrial furniture company, and he turned out to be a good salesman. He made it his goal to become the top regional salesperson in the company, and he met it. "Having already lost a job, I knew that opportunity doesn't last forever and I'd better take advantage of it," he said. Selling industrial furniture doesn't sound sexy, and it wasn't, until the company landed the U.S. mil-itary as a client. "Reagan was spending a lot on defense, and bases were being renovated, and it turned out to be very lucrative," he said. "In 1998, I cashed out and bought a house." He also bought some other businesses along the way, including a collection agency, and seemed to have made out quite well. (I called him for an update almost two years after we first met. He had recently started a company called Toolboxes and More, which sells indus-trial equipment online, and he's as obsessed as ever. Within a few days of our follow-up conversation, I received in the mail a Tool-boxes and More duffel bag and press kit and a letter from Marsala wishing me luck.)

We moved our conversation into the main house, and as we talked Marsala walked me down a hall of framed photographs, many of them of his apparently legendary backyard parties, often showing guests acting as giant chess pieces. One shindig had a Venetian theme, complete with a gondola, which, in one photo, was being navigated in the pool by the largest shareholder of General Electric. "He collects army tanks," Marsala said, shaking his head and chuckling, as if the man collected scrimshaw or hermit crabs. "He has about two hundred and fifty of them, right up the street."

When it was time to begin our listening tour of Atherton, I followed Marsala into the garage.

"I don't think it's going to rain anymore, so I thought we'd take this," he said. There, in the garage, was a mint-condition, blazing-red Ferrari Mondial convertible. I nodded in agreement: we should take this. As I jackknifed myself into the street-scraping passenger seat, Marsala told me that the car had appeared in the 1992 film *Scent of a Woman,* in the scene where Al Pacino, playing a blind man, begs a Ferrari dealer to let his assistant, played by Chris O'Donnell, take him for a spin through Manhattan.

"You mean it was the same model as this one?" I asked.

"No," Marsala replied, smiling. "It was this exact *car.*"

My ass. Pacino's ass. Same seat.

Atherton.

Take Your Mind Off the Money — You'll Earn More

"All the people I know who have a lot of money are all still working."

Around the country, the more doors I knocked on and the more people I interviewed, the more adept I became at determining which people merely had a lot of money (all of them) and which were truly loaded—waterfront, courtside, family foundation loaded (a slightly smaller group). Of the latter, many expressed the same impassioned sentiment about what their motivation for success was: it was *not*, they assured me, the money.

Sure, I thought. *Easy for you to say. You could buy a Stradivarius with the money in your couch cushions.* Claiming that financial gain isn't a motivating factor sounds a little like a lottery winner saying he only bought the ticket to support his local 7-Eleven. But the fact is, I believed them. Every one of them. By the time I completed my journey, it had been drilled into my head that if extreme wealth is your only goal, you will probably never become extremely wealthy. Milking a job you love for all it's worth, however — now you're getting somewhere.

Mayor Marsala had scheduled an interview with Dave Dollinger, a real estate titan in Silicon Valley. The Ferrari skimmed across the rain-darkened roads of Atherton and neighboring Palo Alto like a water bug until we arrived at Dollinger's office, windblown.

Dollinger was in the extreme-wealth echelon. That's my educated guess, anyway. When I asked him earnestly how he planned to pay his kids' tuition and whether he had any savvy advice about affording college, he stared at me for a long moment as if I had asked what my own name was. Suddenly I felt very naive, but I didn't know why. Then he said, "I'm going to write a check." Oh. Right. Of course.

Dollinger was around forty and wore jeans and a polo shirt. His thin brown hair was cropped close, and when he smiled he smiled big, which made him squint. He had been in real estate for twenty years and said he had benefited by embracing patience as a way of life: "I buy to hold, not to sell," he told me. One source of his seemingly preternatural willpower is his keen understanding of one uncomplicated fact about the market in which he operates: "California is a constrained market. There's only one direction prices go."

As we spoke, sitting at a shiny conference table, on a high floor of a building Dollinger owns, sipping bottled water, I sensed that he was impatient with my questions about getting ahead and earning money. His body language and tone suggested that I was missing the point. Instead of offering aphorisms about working hard or smart investing, he told me about the first building he had ever bought, an undertaking that at first sounded to me like a young kid's lucky gambit.

"I had just graduated from college, and I lived with my parents," he said. "I could barely pay my rent. I went in on the building with five friends from school—we all signed on as general partners. We could have turned around and sold it and bought a house, but we didn't sell it. I still have it. There's this great quote that I love that goes something like, 'If you sell things quickly, you get rich. But if you hold on to them, you get wealthy.'"

Not that Dollinger knew that at the time. What he did figure out very quickly was that he loved this business of buying and selling buildings. "When I was financing that first building I bought with my friends, the guy at San Jose National Bank said he gave me the loan because, he said, 'You were so excited about it.'"

For Dollinger, the biggest thrill seemed to be the deal, not the building itself, and to this day he is, or appears to be, obsessed with engineering and executing deals. Keep in mind that in this chapter I mean *obsession* in the best possible way: a fulfilling, inspiring, invigorating, and consuming interest in something. Closing a land deal is fun, and it's something Dollinger is very good at; each successful transaction fertilizes his desire to do another. The excitement he felt as a college grad in those first negotiations never faded, no matter how big the deals got. Whatever ignited that fervor—the thrill of ownership, the frisson of negotiation, the exciting prospect of long-term growth—satisfied Dollinger each time but also made him hungry again.

And after that first deal, there was no windfall to revel in. He hadn't actually made any money. He had only made the *deal*. And he loved it.

Jason Zweig, author of *Your Money and Your Brain*, explained to me why the anticipation of success often excites us more than success itself: "Anticipation is really critical to survival. If anticipating a reward didn't feel at least as good as getting the reward, we would never really know what was rewarding. Anticipation is evolution's way of guiding us toward reward, and it tends to be more intense than the actual gain. Evolutionary psychology is all about extrapolating the imagination backwards in time. Imagine our ancestors squatting in caves somewhere in southern Europe. If the thought of capturing the mastodon didn't feel better than *actually* capturing it turned out to feel, they never would have gone out to capture it. It was the thrill of the hunt, the thrill of the chase—terms that we still have in our collective language."

After Dollinger and I spoke, I found a news report stating that his company, Dollinger Properties, had bought almost a million square feet of commercial research and development space in Silicon Valley in the previous two years, long after the dot-com bust. He continued to see great promise in the area, even if others didn't, and the pure speculation of it excited him. "It doesn't matter how much money you have. All the people I know who have a lot of money are all still working," he said. "I don't go out and do another real estate deal right now because I want to make a dollar. I do it because it's fun, and I like putting deals together. I don't go home at night and say, 'Oh, boy, I made two dollars today.' The driver isn't the money."

He let the last sentence hang for a minute, almost glaring as I wrote it down, as if to emphasize that his pursuit of the thrill of the deal was fueled by something much, much deeper than profit. I believed him.

Dave Dollinger's argument was that the truest form of financial success is the lagniappe—the unexpected bonus. This is an oversimplification, but to make a fortune without *trying* to make a fortune seems like the only way to be both wealthy and happy. I'm not saying that the people I interviewed were indifferent toward the money they had made—they seemed to enjoy it very much. Who wouldn't? It's nice to be able to write a simple check for your child's college tuition and to build a gargantuan villa because it's your wife's dream to live in one. Part of what makes a good business idea good, after all, is its potential to bring in some dough, and profit is not a bad measure of whether anyone is actually buying your goods or using your services. What's important, though, is that you benefit from what you're doing in ways that are more spiritual—I guess that's the word—than remunerative.

Don't Plan a Career – Plan a Life

"All I wanted to do was paint and sculpt. The hell with everything else."

In Paradise Valley, Arizona—median income $157,478, average home value $1,070,460, average net worth $1,356,956—I pulled into the parking lot of El Chorro's bar around five o'clock on a Friday afternoon. The pimply kid working the front desk at my generic businessman's hotel had suggested that the place might be a good spot to meet people for my research—a way to continue working into the evening, when it was too late in the day to knock on doors. Plus, there was the added benefit of it being a purveyor of spirits, which might make the initial introductions a little easier.

As the clerk had promised, El Chorro's was happening. Most of the patrons were old-timers, longtime residents of Paradise Valley, the seasoned upper crust of Scottsdale. Everyone was loose. They bought each other drinks and sang show tunes, slurring a little, around a piano off in a corner. The half-light of an early spring sunset made the dark wood paneling look chalky. Within ten minutes I had met the mayor of Paradise Valley, two tables' worth of people, and Harland Young—eighty-two years old, black motorcycle jacket, sipping something, holding court at a round table in the middle of the room. The guy who introduced us told me that Young had once competed in the Mr. America contest. "I finished in ninth place," Young interjected loudly. I skipped my spiel and asked him what the best financial decision he ever made was. Without hesitating, he shouted above the jangly piano, "Enlisting." I leaned in, and I must have looked confused. He elaborated: "Going to art school was—that was a big investment. I enlisted in World War Two. I wouldn't have been able to go to art school if I hadn't enlisted. All I wanted to do was paint and sculpt. The hell with everything else."

If I understood him correctly, Young had enlisted in the Army Air Corps with the ulterior goal of financing his art school tuition. This struck me as a particularly obsessive way to pursue one's calling but also rather brilliant. He went on to become a successful artist, graduating in 1951 from the Art Center College in Los Angeles, an edgy, well-regarded hive of creativity and innovation founded in 1930. Young worked for an advertising agency for a while, as an illustrator, before opening his own studio in 1956. In 1970, he was commissioned to paint a portrait of

John Wayne, which Young personally presented to Wayne. He ran a horse ranch in addition to painting, sculpting, and drawing, but in 1976 he sold that and has been making art ever since, full time. He even got into painting those commemorative plates you see advertised, which brings in quite a bit of money. Young knew what he wanted. It wasn't complicated. Obsession never is.

Obsession Makes You Work Harder

"I wasn't your average art dealer who wore a little black dress and three strings of pearls. It wasn't a hobby. I wanted to be independent."

Newport, Tennessee, is a long way from Palm Beach, Florida. Geographically, for one thing, but also in every other way. Fifty miles west of Knoxville as the crow flies, snug by the North Carolina border, Newport sounds like a tough place to escape. According to city-data.com, the town's 7,400 residents post a median household income of $20,000, almost half the state average in a state that doesn't rank high nationally, and 6 percent of the adult population hold a bachelor's degree.

On my list of the top one hundred wealthiest ZIP codes, meanwhile, Palm Beach (33480), a sixteen-mile-long shoal separated from the mainland by the Intracoastal Waterway, ranked number seventy-six. Its residents, many of whom are retired (the median age of its residents is sixty-six, making it the most elderly town on the list), had an average net worth of $1,386,837, and their homes were valued at an average of $838,024.

Rena Holman grew up in Newport, Tennessee, and now she lives, for part of each year, in Palm Beach. Her other home is Park Avenue in the 90s, on Manhattan's Upper East Side, a wealthy part of a wealthy neighborhood in a wealthy city. I arrived at the door of her Florida home late in the afternoon, and a cool, salty sweat had dampened my shirt collar. I retucked, patted down my humidified hair, and rang the bell. Holman answered, wearing exercise clothes and holding back a golden retriever. She said she had been out walking the dog and asked me to wait outside while she changed, which was great, because it gave my perspiration a few minutes to dry in the slight breeze. Eventually she reappeared, inviting me in. She was petite and had wispy blond hair, and she wore black velvety slippers and a black silk robe. The dog now played in the small in-ground swimming pool in the backyard.

"Newport was about as bad as it gets," she told me, lowering her voice a little. She had a lovely southern accent; the word "gets" grew to two long, elegant syllables. We were sitting opposite each other on pillowy sofas covered with fabric as soft as a queen's hand. The floors were polished marble, and I'm pretty sure the staircase had been carved from one huge solid piece of stone. The upstairs hallways crisscrossed like a catwalk over the ground level. Faux columns were built into the living room walls, with oil paintings hung in between. The house, which was contemporary with Tuscan flourishes, sat on a corner lot across the street from the Atlantic Ocean. The Kennedy family's compound was about fifty yards away. (Why is every Kennedy home always referred to as a compound? I don't know, but I'm not going to break precedent now.)

Holman told me about her long career as an art dealer. Her deeper goal—the thing that inspired her to turn her love of art into a livelihood—was a desire for financial independence. Her life in the art business had begun as just a job she wanted to see if she liked, in a place that sounded to me like an improbable setting for a young woman to be swept into the world of buying and selling fine art: Memphis. "In school I picked up subjects—painting, art history, things like that, but then when I got involved in it I saw that I didn't really have the talent to paint like the artists whose work I would end up carrying," she said.

In her first job in the art field, she worked for an aficionado named Hugo Dixon, who had made his fortune in the cotton business. As Dixon's apprentice, Holman learned how to sell fine art to the southern upper class, many of whom, like Dixon, had cotton money. She told me Dixon's gallery was the first of its kind in Memphis, and it did extremely well. (Upon his death in 1974, Dixon donated his estate to the city; it is now the Dixon Gallery and Gardens, a prominent institution and showplace for a respected permanent collection of paintings.)

Having left home at a young age, Holman had found a field she loved, and she worked hard to learn as much about it as she could. "I read books, I saw how other people acted—I had a thirst for knowledge," she said. "Newport is a beautiful little town right in the mountains, and the landscape is beautiful, but there was no industry there. What I saw at a young age was that it was going to be a hard life if I had stayed there. It was much better for me to work my way through school—I was a good student—and associate myself with people like the Dixons."

Early on, Holman married a man who had a lot of money, but it didn't last—the marriage or the money. "You know how it goes: the first generation made it, and the second and third generations spent it," she said, frowning a little. "He wasn't a good manager." The marriage was a setback. From that experience, Holman took the lesson that nothing in life is certain. The man had money, but, under the circumstances, that didn't bring anything like security. "You never knew what might happen tomorrow," she said. "I wanted to be in a position that no matter who I was married to, I would have something for myself."

Holman's father, a contractor, had lived through the Great Depression, and from him Holman learned never to be complacent—wealthy husband or not. "I just wanted to make a living," she said. "I had married a prominent man, but I wanted to do something self-satisfying. I wasn't your average art dealer who wore a little black dress and three strings of pearls. It wasn't a hobby. I wanted to be independent. I wanted a place in the community, a place in life. I wanted some dignity, to be able to support myself. And my income in the art business, eventually, ended up being significant."

I asked Holman what Dixon had taught her, and what advice she would pass along to anyone starting off in a business—any business. Without hesitating, she replied, "He taught me patience, and that's something anyone in any business needs." In her early days as a dealer, Holman was tireless. She encouraged unknown artists, cold-called prospective clients, and searched endlessly for new talent. She also swept the floors and sweated out the cycle of chores that follows any small businessperson from one day to the next, because there's no one else to do them. She may have married into some money once, but to emphasize her self-reliance to me she contrasted herself with Donald Trump, a longtime Palm Beach luminary: "Trump started out with money. That wasn't my luck. I hung my own shows—and you can imagine little me trying to hang a great big painting. It's about taking out your own trash and things like that. Then, eventually, you have the exhibition and you throw on the little black dress and the three strings of pearls."

What I learned most from Holman was never to assume anything about anyone. Here she was hanging out at her luxurious beachside home, surrounded by fine art. But go with her back in time a few years, and she'll show you curiosity, passion, sweat, and fierce independence. Had she not become obsessed with the idea of financial autonomy, an obsession that was inextricably wrapped up in an equally fervent love for art, she might never have discovered the business of buying and selling art. I'm sure Newport, Tennessee, is a fine place, but she seemed more comfortable sitting on her expensively comfortable sofa in Palm Beach.

Incidentally, Holman did remarry. Her career, while very successful, wasn't the only source of income funding this lifestyle. How did she meet her husband? He bought a painting from her.

If You Look Forward to Going to Work, That's a Good Sign

"Luck? Luck is when you're at your desk until four a.m. every night, and a few years later you look up and your broker tells you you're worth a few million dollars."

In Austin, Texas, I found proof that the combination of work, passion, intelligence, and youthful single-mindedness can lead to a good, old-fashioned payday—but only if the proportions of all the ingredients are right. You can work very hard at something your heart's not in, but sooner or later you'll lose that drive. You can be passionate about the idea of a particular goal—opening your own Pilates studio or becoming the vice president for corporate communication or writing a book—but the idea will remain a dream, something *other* people do, if you don't do anything about it. And you can be passionate and work hard, but if you don't use your brain, you might end up channeling your heroic efforts in the wrong direction. That's where the need for obsessive focus comes in. It forces you to use your brain.

Toward the end of a long, hot Saturday, I drove my rental car slowly down a quiet street that ran next to the Colorado River, looking for an inconspicuous place to park. I found the stretch of riverside homes after having only a vague idea of where I was going; I'd seen a sign that said WATERFRONT and pointed down a road wending through thick woods, so I took a shot, reasoning that I might find prime real estate at the bottom.

A note about my rates of success in various towns around the country: Many people have asked me what the friendliest place I visited was, the town where I scored the highest ratio of good interviews to doors knocked on. But I always resist answering because no matter what I say, it won't be true. Granted, I had to go to more than sixty houses in Seattle to get three good conversations, and in Austin I knocked on just ten doors and got four good interviews. But does that mean Austin is empirically friendlier than Seattle? Of course not. It means that in Austin, on the streets where I was, and at the time of day I happened to be there, more people were home. Maybe in Seattle there were five fascinating people who would have loved to talk to me for hours, but two had run out to the grocery store, two were out back by their swimming pools and didn't hear the doorbell, and one heard me knocking and yearned to talk to me but had accidentally locked himself in the attic and ended up eating ants for two days, until his wife returned from a business trip and let him out.

Still, my luck in Austin was truly phenomenal. I logged a few hard miles on my loafers, but nowhere else did I have more success at fewer houses. My only regret on the trip was the side dish of very spicy serrano pepper-and-cheese spinach I ordered with my plate of brisket and ribs at Stubb's Bar-B-Q before setting out. It tasted great at the time, but it was perhaps inadvisable considering how I would be spending the rest of my afternoon.

Breaking my earlier pledge not to generalize about any city, I can't help correlating my good luck in Austin to some umbrella trait—in this case, the spirit of ambition that has marked the city's ascension over the last couple of decades. The Dell Corporation was an instigator of Austin's economic expansion, but all around it, other, smaller companies have reaped the benefits of healthy venture capital infusions and an abundance of technological talent. Plus, technology companies don't thrive on computer experts alone. They need salespeople, marketers, HR departments, contractors to build their offices, and all the other supporting players that can transform a regular city into a hub of commerce. I don't know a lot about the intricacies of Austin's business development, but I do know this: Three individuals granted me extended interviews in Austin, and all three of them spoke effusively of their good fortune to live and work in a city that has a culture of ambition, entrepreneurialism, and hard work. In no other place I visited did even one person mention the town as a direct contributor to his or her success.

I followed the WATERFRONT sign down a road into a valley. At the bottom was a strip of homes hugging the banks of the Colorado. As in Sandy Springs, Georgia, where I found the Dwyers' replica Italian villa, this was a street of modest, mid-twentieth-century houses coexisting with larger structures built more recently. Just a few were what you might call McMansions, but it was still obvious which lots the new money had landed on. The paint was fresher, the roofs were newer, the landscaping was more calculated.

I visited precisely one home on this street—it was about half past five by the time I made it into the valley, so I didn't have much time to ring doorbells before the dinner hour—and there

I found a cheerful woman of around forty who spoke to me for twenty minutes on the steps in front of her home. It was actually two homes that she and her husband had purchased and conjoined, transforming them into a V-shaped riverfront mansion. To get to her doorbell I walked over a tiny bridge that spanned a lily-pad pond directly in front of the door.

"Well, we both worked for Dell," she told me right off the bat, smiling and giving a little shrug. "There were only nine hundred employees at the time." That was long before the company took up permanent residence on the Fortune 500 list. Today, Dell employs more than sixty-five thousand people.

She was small and slim and had very short blond hair and green eyes; she wore a pink T-shirt, pink floral-print pants, and pink polish on her toenails. She said she had worked in sales and asked that I not use her name (this seemed to have something to do with her not wanting to draw attention to the fact that Dell was the source of her wealth or the fact that she was wealthy at all— remember Mark Banta, the health care entrepreneur in Austin who said you never know who in town is worth seven figures or eight?). But she spoke unguardedly about how she and her husband, an engineer, thrived at the company Michael Dell founded in 1984 with, as the Dell Web site puts it, "$1,000 in startup capital and an unprecedented idea" to build relationships directly with customers.

"Michael Dell was a great person to work for. But it's not like *every* employee who was there at the beginning ended up making out this well," she said, nodding at the spectacular house from which she had just emerged. I asked her if she felt she had been lucky to be in the right place at the right time. Her answer: "Luck? Luck is when you're at your desk until four a.m. every night, chasing deals and trying to come up with the next big thing, and a few years later you look up and your broker tells you you're worth a few million dollars."

This is an important point: Anyone can find herself at the right place at the right time. But if you don't recognize that or work hard to take advantage of it—or if you're lazy or unfocused—you can be at the best possible place at the best possible time and still end up making $70,000 instead of $700,000. Or, like the lady in pink said, a few million.

The Dell Lady attributed her ability to work so hard in part to youthful ignorance. "You don't know what you don't know, so you just forge ahead with moxie and whatever smarts you've got. And I'll tell you what: it's probably a blessing that you don't know a lot of things, because if you did you'd be scared. So a lot of us back then were just eager little beavers because we didn't know any better. You just don't know what square you're going to land on, so you keep working and keep working," she said.

There is great virtue in being young and clueless about the future, because you have no reference point. You just work as hard as you can, because you haven't yet figured out how much you can afford to slack off and get away with, so you don't slack off at all. If you're smart, you obsess over your work while you have the energy to do so. The result, you hope, is that you are rewarded for your efforts and that your brain learns that hard work equals prizes. And thus begins a lifelong cycle of never slacking off and periodically socking away untold piles of cash into your bank account.

(That, incidentally, is a concise interpretation of my general philosophy of success—oversimplified, but not by much. In fact, you could cut out the preceding paragraph and put it in your wallet, and you'd probably do okay. It wouldn't take up much space, so there'd be plenty of room for lots of money.)

Discover Love Through Immersion

"I work longer than most people because I think it's fun.
I don't come home and watch TV at night. If you work twice as hard,
you're going to be twice as successful."

I had this weird thing happen in a few cities. It usually went like this: The sun was low in the sky, my feet were swollen and throbbing in my loafers. I wondered if it was too late in the day to knock on a door. Four-thirty, five o'clock—around that time on a Saturday that people do stuff. They finish up the yard work. They get ready for an evening out. They nap or start preparing dinner.

So, I would always say to myself, You've got one more house. One try. I would make it a little game: Get in the car (no time to spare for walking) and drive until you spot the house. *The* house, the one beautiful dwelling where (a) it looks like someone is home, and (b) it looks like that person will be friendly, gregarious, fascinating, and insightful. A person who will leave me assured that my trip to this city was a success. A long shot, basically, because I had nothing to go on but the number of lights I saw on inside and my ever-improving instincts. By the time I found The House, parked, and went through my spiel at the door, ten minutes would have passed—just enough to make it too late to try another. The stakes were high.

But here's the thing: it worked almost every time. In Austin, where I found the Dell Lady at five-thirty. In Westport, Connecticut, where I saw a beautiful winter sunset from a retired CEO's waterfront living room. In New York City, where I was on foot but thought to myself, *One more block,* and I met a great couple.

And it worked in Cleveland. Shaker Heights, actually, where I steered my rental car quickly after a long, educational afternoon in Gates Mills. It was going on five o'clock, during the stretch of winter when streetlights start to flicker on at four-thirty against a rich, smoky sky. But Shaker Heights is a well-known haven for old and new money, so I sped there, Google map printout pressed hard against the wheel, knowing I would have time to knock on precisely one door.

And I nailed it.

The dog saw me first, a beautiful Akita, wagging its tail. Behind it, a woman emerged from the dim depths of a sprawling Tudor house. I chose the house because it looked like a castle. A single pentagonal tower rose, off-center, in the front, studded with crenellations and, like the rest of the place, built of solid stone. A thick slate roof capped everything, like the heavy lid of a treasure chest. I would soon learn that the house wasn't always Tudor style; the original owners, at one point, had imported dark, Tudor wood paneling for the interior and added the Tudor details to the outside so that it would match the new interior. (Rich people!)

The dog's owner turned out to be Robin Schachat, forties, hair in a bun, purple eyeglasses, blue jeans, fleece. I had barely got my spiel out before she was inviting me in for coffee. Coffee was always a good sign. It usually promised a long conversation. Coffee meant hospitality, it meant no rush, and it meant a measure of trust and acceptance. Coffee meant a person was willing to see where this conversation took them.

She led me through the foyer, past two converging spiral staircases, and down a long, paneled hall. In its scale and beauty, the interior gave off the vibe of some hallowed corridor at Oxford or Yale. We passed an office, where her husband, Andy, was on the phone and waved, unsurprised, as if I were an expected guest. In the kitchen, which had been designed long ago for use by servants, Robin had one of those one-cup coffee makers, into which you insert individual pods and a few seconds later have a cup of steaming joe.

"All I have left is the gingerbread flavor," she said, pulling a half gallon of organic skim milk from the fridge and setting it next to the sugar bowl.

Robin showed me a servants' call-board in the kitchen—a kind of legend for the intercom system, with names of rooms written next to the different buttons. This is when I found out that the house had been built in 1908 by M. J. and O. P. Van Sweringen, two brothers who had essentially created the town of Shaker Heights. They had added the "Van" to their surname, supposedly to sound more aristocratic. You could see it written in on the servants' board, squeezed carefully but awkwardly in front of "Sweringen." The brothers had purchased land for many homes and eventually financed a commuter rail line into Cleveland. The town spread over empty land under the brothers' careful watch, and from the beginning it was designed as a clubby suburb for Cleveland's upper class. "People may not live longer in Shaker Village—but they live better" was an early town slogan, before the Van Sweringens enhanced the town's already-elite image by changing the word *Village* to *Heights*.

Andy joined us in the dining room, which was larger than my entire apartment back in Manhattan. Avalanche, the dog, brought me toys, and my coffee sat untouched on a stack of paperback books as I took notes.

The Schachats had moved to Shaker Heights only recently, from Baltimore. The exquisiteness of the house, Robin said, had only added excitement to the move. "I made a trip out here first, to look at houses," she said. "I walked into this one, and I thought, I'm in trouble. It was like the house reached out and said, 'You're here! Thank God.' Andy came out a few months later, and we looked at a bunch of places, including this one. At dinner that night, he said, 'Well, we saw seven houses and a work of art today.'" They bought the work of art.

The Schachats were kind and seemed humble, and they imbued their big house with a warmth it might not have had with other owners. Andy is an ophthalmologist, and they had settled in Baltimore after he attended medical school at Johns Hopkins, where he eventually ended up teaching for twenty-two years. Andy's hair winged out on the sides a little, and his graying beard softened his handsomely angled face. His eyes were intense, and he wore a small, patient smile as I asked my questions about buying and selling houses, about whether or not he and Robin were planners by nature, and about what advice he had for people just starting out.

Finally he said, "What you're really getting at, I think, is how do you make a lot of money. If there was a recipe for that, then everyone would do it. If you could write that down . . ."

He stopped, and I nodded, a tiny bit deflated. I thought to myself, *But don't you see? I've talked to a lot of people. I am writing down the recipe. I think. I'm trying.*

Then Andy, who grew up in Manhattan and had held fast to that city's frank but not unfriendly manner, shifted in his chair. He looked at me hard, as if to say, "All right, you want to know what I think?"

"My father was an ophthalmologist," he began. "I didn't even know how to *spell* it. But we had a family ritual, where every night at the dinner table we'd go around asking everyone, 'What did you do today, and did you enjoy it?' My father always sounded like he really enjoyed what he did. So I drifted down that path, because I knew that a sure thing existed. He loved it so much and spoke so highly of it that it just seemed obvious to me. I knew other people enjoyed other things, but I had this firsthand knowledge, like proof, that ophthalmology was good. I had evidence."

Schachat did not have evidence of his own future love of the study of the human eye, however. But in a sense, from his first day of medical school, he was pursuing more than the knowledge of how to care for diseased retinas. He was pursuing the kind of happiness he had seen in his father every night at supper. He was chasing satisfaction, and he already knew where to find it—or, at least, he knew the place where his father had found it. Turns out it was his thing too—he loved ophthalmology, just as he thought he would. And then something remarkable happened: Schachat found himself not only trying to replicate his father's happiness but to improve on it. He spends his spare time writing professional articles, attending conferences, and generally devoting himself to enhancing his own understanding of a field that he has clearly already mastered. He made it a part of him. Schachat spends an inordinate amount of time not only on his job's considerable requirements, but on extracurricular activities he seeks out with the same spirit of ambition as a kid trying to get into a good college. He has written or coauthored five books and more than two hundred articles in his field. He is the editor-in-chief of *Ophthalmology,* the journal of the American Academy of Ophthalmology, where he also sits on the board of trustees. He moved to Cleveland to become the vice chair for clinical affairs at the Cleveland Clinic's Cole Eye Institute; he specializes in an area of ophthalmology that treats diseased retinas by using lasers and drugs instead of conventional scalpel surgery. The clinic's Web site calls him "a world-renowned expert in treating retinal disorders."

I took a sip of my now-cool gingerbread coffee and waved an arm at the grand, cavernous house surrounding us — proof, in a way, that success is the result of going after something you know will make you happy. I said something like, "This is an amazing house. Looks like you were right about enjoying what your father did." Schachat blinked, smiled, and told me about a conference he had attended recently. Someone had turned to him during an interminable meeting, offered a hint of a sarcastic smile, and said, "Isn't this fun?" Schachat didn't answer out loud, but he thought to himself, *Well, yeah, it is fun.*

Sometimes, you don't need to have an original idea to rise above everyone else. You don't have to invent the world's next bubble wrap or MP3 player or Post-it Note. Schachat didn't invent ophthalmology. But he liked it, then he loved it, then it became a part of his soul, so he became the best ophthalmologist he knew how to be. The advice here might seem easy to follow on the surface, but it requires extra self-awareness: If you've found a job that you like, by all means, *cherish* it. Feel lucky. Use all of your working energy to milk the job for everything it's worth, both creatively and financially. Explore facets of it that other people wouldn't think of. Write journal articles. Seek out and serve on committees that interest you. Freelance. Blog. Whatever. What you'll find, I think, is that your career will feed off itself, becoming bigger, more satisfying — and, ultimately, more lucrative. I wondered to myself whether Schachat's career would have been the same if he had gone into ophthalmology knowing nothing about it — say, if his father had been a grocer or an architect. It doesn't matter.

"I get tremendous satisfaction from helping people," he said. "Success is basically about enjoying your work. I work longer than most people because I think it's fun. I guess I don't come home and watch TV at night. I come home and do ophthalmol-ogy-related things. If you work twice as hard, you're going to be twice as successful."

Turn Fear into Passion

....

**"In my opinion, a successful business has little to do with the idea.
It's almost entirely about the person pursuing the idea."**

....

We are not supposed to want money. Materialism, we learn at a young age, is frowned upon. This attitude does not seem altogether compatible with a system of capitalism, but as a code to live by it is probably—and theoretically—an admirable way to go: do not do anything solely for money, and do not covet material goods for their own sake. As Ralph Waldo Emerson wrote, "Great men are they who see that the spiritual is stronger than any material force, that thoughts rule the world."

True enough. This is also true: unless you are a monk or a hunter-gatherer living in the Canadian subarctic, you generally need money to buy food, clothing, and shelter. Clarence Odd-body, the angel who is trying to earn his wings in the classic 1946 film *It's a Wonderful Life,* casually tells the forlorn George Bailey (Jimmy Stewart), "We don't use money in heaven." To which Bai-ley retorts, "Oh, that's right, I keep forgetting. Comes in pretty handy down here, bub."

The question is, how much money do we need? And is it okay to want more than we need? Sure it is. Not to have to worry about money is the most basic luxury since the advent of wam-pum. Money may not buy happiness, but if sailing a boat makes you happy, you do need to be able to buy the boat. Let's not forget that at the end of Frank Capra's holiday fable, George Bailey's friends and family parade through his living room with heartwarming expressions of love and support in the form of . . . money, apparently the only thing that can save him from ruin.

As Bailey found out, whether or not money can buy happiness, it certainly gets you another intangible, important asset: security. The final story in this chapter is about one man's remarkable pursuit of the ineluctable happiness that comes with financial security. Which means, I suppose, that money *can* buy happiness, through the transitive property of equality: if $a = b$, and $b = c$, then $a = c$, where a is money, b is financial security, and c is happiness. That concludes the math portion of this book.

I came across this story on my trip to Florida, but it had been right under my nose for years. I needed a place to stay near Palm Beach, one of the ZIP codes on my list of the hundred richest, so I called an old family friend, Scott Zdanis. He grew up a few towns away from me in Connecticut and now lives in Miami. Zdanis is doing well in life. One night while I was there, he treated his girlfriend and me to a sushi dinner at Nobu, in Miami Beach, then to drinks at the Shore Club. We headed back to the waterfront house he rents, where in the garage he showed me his Ford GT (MSRP: $167,500) and his Mercedes SL65 604-horsepower biturbo V-12 (MSRP: $191,575). We played a little Ping-Pong on the deck, then, as we reclined on comfortable chairs in his living room, the Florida winds blowing in off the water, it hit me: Zdanis belongs in the book! Technically, I did knock on his door, after the airport taxi dropped me off. And he's the only person I know who's around my age and runs a multimillion-dollar company, so it seemed silly not to include his story. Here's a guy who once showed up at my parents' house driving a brand new Porsche

911 Turbo when he was twenty-three years old. Then came the Hummer H1, and the Lamborghini a couple of years after that. When my brother got married in New York City a few years ago, we ended up drinking single malt scotch late one night on the deck of Scott's seventy-foot, twenty-three-hundred-horsepower, five-bedroom yacht, which his personal captain had docked at a pier on the West Side of Manhattan for the weekend.

Ask Zdanis how he scored any of this stuff, and he'll tell you he's just following his plan.

Zdanis didn't come from money. His family was far from poor, but money was always an issue. Worrying about income didn't seem like much fun to him. His parents both sold insurance and worked other jobs, and Zdanis liked the idea of collecting regular income for very little work. One of his father's gigs was with a company in the credit-card-processing industry. When any new business—from Home Depot to a mom-and-pop hardware store—wants to accept credit cards from its customers, it must first purchase the machines you swipe your card through, and then pay a fee for each transaction.

Traditionally, the business worked like this: Joe's Hardware Store wants to start accepting credit cards from its customers. Joe calls Bill Middleman, who sells Joe a card swiper for $1,000. Bill then sets up an account for Joe with Big Processing Corp. For each credit-card transaction at his store, Joe must pay BPC a small percentage, of which Bill gets a minuscule percentage, if any. BPC can pay Bill Middleman as poorly as it pleases, because his contract doesn't give him the right to take the Joe's Hardware Store account to another processor—so there is no competition among processors. But Bill seems satisfied to make his money up front, when he sells Joe the swiper, which he has marked up more than

300 percent. After that, he barely sees another dime from Joe, instead looking for the next merchant to whom he can sell a $300 machine for $1,000.

Zdanis saw a flawed system juiced with opportunity. Why shouldn't the middleman receive any of the residual income? Who cared about making another few hundred bucks by marking up the card-swiping machines? The value was in the accounts. "It seemed kind of obvious, and now in hindsight people say, 'Hmm, that was obvious,' " he said. "You see it in other industries all the time. Internet service providers aren't trying to nail you for a thousand dollars up front; they just want the twenty bucks a month. I thought, Sell the machines cheaper and collect the fees for each transaction. But even my biggest supporters told me I was going to dig myself into a hole with that model. They said, 'You can't sell the machines at cost and run a profitable business. You're going to spend so much money acquiring accounts that you're never going to make it back on the residuals.' And I said, 'What are you talking about? The money's not in the equipment. It's a *residual* business! How do you not understand that?' And while yes, there was a time early on when I had a lot of debt because I had to front for the equipment, those days are gone, and now I've got all these merchants that I attracted with that equipment offer."

His next question: Why shouldn't the company that sold the account—the middleman—be able to take it to a different processor if it's not getting the terms it wants?

So now Zdanis, who was all of twenty-two when he started Merchant Warehouse in 1998, has turned the credit-card-processing business upside down, primarily with those two innovations: First, he sells the card-swiping equipment at cost—a boon for the business owner—and focuses only on residuals. Second, he introduced the concept of portability of accounts, meaning that he, as the new middleman, can take any of his accounts to any of the major processors in the industry at any time—the very processors who pay him his residuals every month. "I'm in the driver's seat. I can do business with anyone I want to," Zdanis said. "Merchants call me wanting to set up accounts, and I can send them anywhere. So are you going to get the business or not? If I don't put the big processing companies in that position, they'll take advantage of me. Or, maybe they won't exactly take advantage of me, but they won't give me a super-out-of-this-world deal if they don't have to. Why would they? But because we've made the accounts portable, the processors negotiate."

So now, when Joe's Hardware Store sells a gallon of paint, Merchant Warehouse—who sold Joe his credit-card equipment at cost, sees to it that all of Joe's Visa, Master Card, Discover, and American Express transactions are processed with those companies, and services the accounts—pays an outside servicer maybe 2 percent to process the transaction but *charges* Joe 2.5 percent, which puts a little money in Zdanis's residual bucket. Merchant Warehouse also charges for customer service—let's say ten dollars, of which it pays four dollars to a subcontractor who actually handles the service, netting six dollars in residuals. Zdanis's company has become a middleman that makes huge amounts of residuals and calls the shots the processors used to call.

"Every month, I basically get paid by these processors who process all this information," says Zdanis. "That's my residual. So I'm just trying to add accounts to that base. It's really an economy-of-scale business; you want to do more and more transactions because you can't go back to your existing customers and say, 'Can I arbitrarily start charging you more now?' "

These days, Merchant Warehouse *adds* at least seventeen hundred new accounts a month and serves a total of around forty thousand businesses.

Not surprisingly, there are some folks in the industry who wish they had come up with Zdanis's innovations first, and they see him as a Goliath. But to have done that, they'd have had to reject the way things had always been done. "I personally have always seen the business world as: there are no rules whatsoever; anything in the world is possible," Zdanis said. "I'm positive to this day it's true. But when you go into business for yourself, people start saying to you, 'You can't do that because it hasn't been done before,' or 'It's not industry standard.' But 'hasn't been done before' or 'not the norm' are just irrelevant to me. Totally irrelevant. It has nothing to do with whether or not it can be done."

The strange thing is, this is exactly what Zdanis wanted to be doing with himself. "I had a plan. As crazy or unusual as this sounds, I specifically wanted to set up a company that does exactly what my company does now. My shorter-term goals were to get self-employed ASAP and to answer to no one. I got some guidance from my father, who had a little agency for Cardservice International, right out of college. I worked out of his office, but I was an independent contractor, so from day one there was no salary, benefits, anything. I was already self-employed, basically," he said. Zdanis had two goals, and he was obsessive about them: he wanted to be independent, and he wanted to have enough money that he wouldn't have to worry about money.

As he puts it, "I did not see security in anything except being paid by me. Going to work for a big company that's been in business for forty years tells you nothing about how long you're going to keep your job. In fact, the bigger the company the scarier, because there's no emotional attachment. If I worked at a small company, with twenty people, I could try to make the CEO feel so bad if he tried to fire me that he wouldn't be able to do it. But you can't do that with big entities. They don't care. And what if I'm into something specialized, and I get canned one day? What if there aren't that many people who do what I do? Now I have to go kiss the butts of those three people in the world who are looking for a guy like me? One of your questions to me was, do I trust people? Generally, I try to set myself up so that it doesn't matter if I trust them or not. Now, that's impossible — you have to trust and depend on certain people — but I try to stay as far to that end of the spectrum as I can."

Zdanis was obsessed with being independently successful from day one, and the most obvious way he could think to measure his success was through the material goods he could afford. He liked expensive toys, so, for starters, he set "one of my silly goals right out of college," and told himself he wanted a Porsche 911 Turbo by the time he was twenty-three. Check. He feels no shame about having a goal like that. "I'm a big fan of goals," he says. "I've always had them. And what seem like stupid materialistic goals — if they get you to the office a little bit earlier each day and to work harder and make more money, they're valuable. I have numerous goals, from tomorrow through five years from now. Having materialistic goals doesn't mean you judge people by stupid things like how many cars they own. It's just what drives *you*. The guy who's not into cars and drives a piece of junk, honestly, gets respect from me because he's definitely smarter than me — driving a Toyota is smarter than driving a hundred-thousand-dollar car, no matter how you cut it. But, you know, I've got this passion for toys, and they motivate me, so fine."

• • •

But what was it that motivated Zdanis to work so hard to avoid subservience in the first place? We'd all like to be independent, we would all like to have a steady income stream made up entirely of residuals, and we would all like to be beholden to no one but ourselves. But usually, a decent job comes along, and we take it, because that's easier than, you know, building an empire out of nothing. Zdanis, however, never entertained the idea of not working for himself—and he set astronomical financial goals so that he would never be in a position where he had to settle for another job. Why?

Fear. That's what set him on his solo course. Fear of putting his fate in someone else's hands. Fear of unpredictability. Fear of not being able to cut it. "I was intimidated by the fact that maybe I didn't have the skills to be one of the best employees out there. I thought I was an excellent entrepreneur, a risk taker, and I had a good feel for capitalism. But at the end of the day, eighty percent of the kids I went to school with got better grades than me. I probably graduated with a two point five. That was mostly laziness, but even if I tried my hardest there still would have been a ton of kids at school getting better grades than me. I knew I wasn't smarter than everybody else, so I had to create security some other way," he said.

He didn't invent the credit-card-processing business, proving that you don't actually have to *come up with* the idea that will propel you to great wealth. You just have to go into your business with the unshakable assumption that it can be revolutionized and that it's up to you to figure out how. "A lot of times, a successful business has little to do with the idea. It's almost entirely about the person pursuing the idea," Zdanis said. "You can make the worst idea in the world work if you have the passion, you make the effort, and you're a good businessperson. People tell me about good ideas. My mother likes stocks, and whenever she hears about a good idea she buys stock in the company. I tell her the idea has nothing to do with whether the company's going to make any money, because you don't know who's executing it. They could be morons. So show me plain vanilla. Show me somebody doing something that's obvious, basic, that makes sense, that people are always going to need, and that's the company that I'm less worried about. We don't have to wonder if there's a need for it."

Obsession can be a scary word. People say the obsessive person is maybe a little single-minded, maybe a little bit insular, maybe even a tiny bit crazy. But real obsession is just a driver, and it's a powerful one. It's more than passion. It's more than focus. It's more than desire. It turns your goal—whether a house, a car, financial independence, the freedom to pursue art—into the only thing you care about. Obsession can clarify your life and help you find what's important to you.

A recent profile of basketball star Kobe Bryant in *Esquire* reported that at the end of every solo practice session, Bryant forces himself to make one hundred shots. Not *take* one hundred shots. *Make* one hundred shots. That's a simple rule, but it helps him stay at or near the top of the NBA's list of high scorers. Bryant is obsessive about his craft.

Here's some advice you can take from him and the people in this chapter: make hard rules that will help you reach your goals. Scott Zdanis figured out exactly how much money he would need to save in order to buy a Porsche 911 Turbo by age twenty-three. Harland Young figured out that enlisting in the Army was the only way he would be able to afford art school. Maybe your rules will be as simple as eating out no more than once a week. (One family in a *Money* magazine story a few years ago stopped buying Q-tips as one of its money-saving tricks. No joke.) Maybe you'll set up an automatic rule, like an online savings account that deducts seventy-five dollars from every paycheck. Trust me, you won't even miss it. Perhaps your rule will be grander: you will send out three résumés each week, and by the end of next year you will have landed a good job in a city where you've always wanted to live, and you will move there.

Whatever your rule is, type it up, print out ten copies, and put them on the fridge, on your TV, next to your bed, in the shower (laminated), in your wallet, on the visor in your car. A little crazy? A little obsessive? Absolutely.

FOUR

THE MYTH OF RISK

It Turns Out That "Big" Gambles Aren't Always So Big

R isk. Risky. Risk taker.

Over and over, on front steps and in living rooms, kitchens, and driveways, rich people talked to me about taking risks. A lot of times, it happened offhandedly: "I don't know; I guess I've taken some risks that have paid off." Or with a shrug and a chuckle, "What can I say? I'm a bit of a risk taker."

But the lack of instruction in these assessments frustrated me. What did they mean, "risk"? It came off as if, maybe a couple of times a year, they went to Atlantic City and bet everything they had on a single spin of the roulette wheel, won, and then bought a bigger motorboat or something. I needed specifics. I needed to understand what risk meant to them. So I started asking two pointed follow-up questions: How dangerous, if you really think about it, were the risks you took? And, how did you know when to go for it, when, exactly, to pull the trigger and make that big move you call "risky"?

The answers to *these* questions came more slowly. The responses were more measured. People's faces would wrinkle up, and they'd false-start a couple of sentences that trailed off, unfinished—stabs at answers to questions they had never really thought about before. I would then lower my pen to my side, a sign that I wanted them to take their time. I didn't want a trite answer. Because isn't that the big question? How do you know when to leave your job so you can follow through on that crazy, invigorating idea that you think about every night while you're trying to fall asleep?

Then, sometimes, if I got lucky, I would witness little epiphanies. These usually came when people realized that the risks they took weren't very dangerous after all. The reason? They had taken them only after preparing extensively for every possible outcome. As Donald Trump once put it: "Work hard to take the gamble out of the gamble." To me, this was heartening news. It meant that these people didn't just put their chips on the right number. They had worked hard to engineer their awesome lifestyles, making their own odds, never betting against the house. It meant it could be done.

Also, most of my interviewees defined the word *risk* in a different way than the rest of us do. To them, buying a lottery ticket is not a risk, nor is skydiving, playing roulette, heli-skiing, or choosing not to buy the optional insurance when you rent a car. Those situations involve chance, but the odds are well known and the variables minimal. Sure, danger might be a concern, but that fact doesn't make the actions risky.

The people I spoke with would define risk more simply: a risk is a bet you've tried to rig.

Heidi Roizen, who I met in the heart of Silicon Valley, worked for years as a venture capitalist, making large investments in relatively unproven companies. Contrary to my previous, uninformed assumptions about venture capital, that didn't mean she spent every day in a state of constant queasiness, making death-defying, billion-dollar decisions. It meant she learned everything she possibly could in order to remove as much uncertainty as possible from any potential investment. "Often when you mention risk, what people think of is the downside—danger," she told me. "That's not the entrepreneurial mind-set. The entrepreneurial mind-set is that risk is the heightened probability that there is a big range of possible outcomes."

Imagine you're playing golf with a friend who tells you about a real estate deal he's getting in on through his sister-in-law. A developer is building a hundred new homes, and while your friend doesn't know much about the project, he swears it's a great opportunity. He's been told that if he buys one of the homes before it's built, he can triple his money by selling it in five years. You think about it. Seems interesting but dicey. You trust this friend. You could swing the up-front investment, but it would be significant. You could dismiss the idea outright and move on to the next tee, or you could pursue it in one of two ways:

1. Go for it, no questions asked. What the hell. This guy is a good friend, pretty smart, and real estate is rarely a bad investment, right?

2. Do extensive research into the project, during which you

find out that the assessed value of the land alone has gone up in each of the past ten years and that the developer has a proven track record of building quality homes. The city is planning to construct a state-of-the-art public school in the neighborhood in five years, new roads are being built near the property, and a high-end supermarket is already going up a mile from the development.

Either way, you're going to look smart in the end. But in the first scenario, you have no idea how good your odds really are, so it's dumb luck. You would have little right to pat yourself on the back. In the second, you have learned as much as you can about the possible outcomes of your investment and have decided that it's a good one. That makes it a smart risk.

When you take any risk, there's a possibility that things could go very well or very badly. Only by studying every imaginable outcome can you know what you're getting into—or at least as much as you can reasonably hope to know.

Speaking of the procurement and disposal of land and houses, ideally at a large profit—otherwise known as the real estate business—it is often thought of, correctly, as risky territory. When you're looking for a house, if you're smart, you study your market obsessively before you even think about calling a broker or opening the Sunday classifieds. How obsessively, exactly? I was about to find out. I had spent all morning roaming some of the most coveted residential real estate in the world—Beverly Hills 90210—before I met a man who'd made a second career of masterfully buying and selling homes. And his wisdom applied to much more than real estate. Even if you never buy or sell a house for the rest of your life, you'll want to hear what he has to say.

First, however, I needed a bite to eat. I had spent a fruitless hour dodging SUVs and BMWs in the steep, thickly populated hills above Sunset Boulevard, taking in the sweet scents and unmistakable sounds of wealth: honeysuckle, chlorine, roses, weed whackers, blessed silence. But I had no idea where I was or what was close by. I wandered along Sunset, a singularly commercial contrail cutting across an otherwise solidly residential expanse, into West Hollywood. When I walked into Duke's, an unfussy diner, the juxtaposition was jarring: it had taken no more than five minutes to walk from streets lined with glitzy mansions to this greasy neighborhood dive. *I hope these rich folks know how good they have it,* I thought.

I sat on a vinyl stool at the counter, reading the framed reviews on the wall as I waited for my cheeseburger and vanilla shake. In most of the write-ups, Duke's was identified as a big hangout for music business honchos; I glanced at a red-bearded guy wearing a black leather jacket in the corner booth, wondering if he had signed Britney Spears once upon a time or maybe produced the last Nine Inch Nails record. A few stools down from me, a man in a suit spoke to the guy working behind the counter. He looked around, leaned in, and said in a low voice that he'd heard that Steven Tyler, the lead singer of Aerosmith, had some sort of serious health problem. He didn't know what it was, but he said it sounded bad. (Sure enough, a few weeks later, the band abruptly canceled the rest of its North American tour due to Tyler's undisclosed illness; he's fine now. Anyway, I heard it first at Duke's.)

Duke's burger, incidentally, was excellent—a charred, well-crusted surface with a pink, juicy center. Fortified, I set out into a section of Beverly Hills below Sunset called the Flats, a plateau separated from the hills by the crease of Sunset Boulevard. The

Flats are bordered by Santa Monica Boulevard, Sunset, Doheny, and Whittier. The neighborhood does not enjoy quite the same prestige that the hills above it do—"That's a different world up there," one Flats resident told me—but the homes themselves are no less spectacular. On some streets, equidistant palm trees tower over the rows of stately houses and neat green lawns, like a movie-set version of a wealthy Los Angeles neighborhood.

Never Stop Being a Student

"No offense to me, but one would not think that I would be where I am.
If I can do it, it means it can be done."

For some reason, in the Flats I encountered the highest number of homes where the owner was in but declined to be interviewed. I chalked this up to random chance, as I had vowed not to ascribe a general personality to any of the neighborhoods I visited. Preconceived notions and generalizations would be unfair, because my sampling of people was sparse and thoroughly unscientific. (It would be easy to say, for example: "I assumed beforehand that Beverly Hills housewives would be generally snotty, and thus I was not surprised that, within ten minutes, two of them waved their bony hands dismissively in my face, mumbled something condescending, and slammed the door," but of course that was just random bad luck and could have happened anywhere. Even though it didn't happen once at the other four hundred and ninety-eight houses in the other eighteen towns I visited.)

But eventually, I met Jeff Weisfeld. His six-foot, auburn-haired, South African wife, Nadine, answered the door, and when she called upstairs to her husband, I heard her tell him I wanted to talk about the house itself. This was actually only part of what I was after, but it was close enough.

Weisfeld, shorter than Nadine, with curly dark hair and excitable eyes, bounded down the stairs wearing black jeans, a golf shirt, and no shoes. From the beginning of our conversation, which spanned an hour and a half, he showed pride in both his home and the fact that he could afford to live in such a safe, beautiful neighborhood. He wasn't bragging—he was genuinely proud. As I would learn, he had earned his address in the Flats by making sound, patient judgments in some risky situations.

"Each street in the Flats has its own tree," he explained as we stood by the curb in the peak afternoon sun. He talked fast. "These are jacaranda trees, and you can see they're all planted in a row going down the street. And there's no parking after a certain time. I'm having a baby-naming here on Sunday, and I have to get a special permit to have cars on the street. There's no parking, and what that means is, there's no crime. See? Having been very skeptical that there was any difference between living in Beverly Hills and anywhere else in L.A., I'm no longer skeptical. You don't know it until you live here. Why are prices in Beverly Hills so ridiculous? The schools. If I'm going to overpay, I'm going to overpay in a place where I don't have to send my kids to private school. You know? And the leaves are cleaned up on a daily basis. Do you see any leaves on the ground?"

Weisfeld's home was built in 1936. He had owned it for about a year, having paid $2.7 million for it the previous spring. I sensed that he was still somewhat surprised that he, Jeff Weisfeld—average-looking, a little soft around the edges, honest, hardworking Jeff Weisfeld—actually lived in this great house in Beverly Hills.

As he explained the circumstances that had brought him here, he seemed to be talking almost as much for his own benefit as for mine. I liked Weisfeld.

"I'm a regular Joe. I'm a produce broker—fruits and vegetables. And yet I live around all these doctors and—over there, the guy in that house is an orthopedic surgeon. A lot of these guys make in a month what I make in a year. Me, I'm the middleman between the farms and the grocery store. I'm up at four-thirty in the morning, and I'm home by one in the afternoon. And this is my ninth home that I've owned and lived in. My child is eight years old, and this is her fourth home. I did it the old-fashioned way. It's kind of the American dream. I just saved all my money," he said.

Weisfeld told me he had made far more money in the risky game of buying and selling houses than he had in his produce company brokering tomatoes and peppers. "Real estate wasn't a plan for me. My business was produce," he said. "When you're twenty-three, you're not thinking about twenty years down the line and what's going to happen—you're not making moves that are going to benefit you in a few years. You're thinking about where you're going to party that weekend. But I found out I had an eye for real estate, so I pursued it on the side. Just like if your business is writing, and you find out you've got an eye for jewelry or antiques or something, then that may be a hobby for you and it might become another source of income. You never know where the next alley is. I've wondered about leaving the produce job and just doing real estate. But I'm not *that* crazy."

As he went on to describe his parade of real estate successes over the years, it became clear that Weisfeld had reaped extraordinary profits from pretty much every house he had ever owned. His secret, he told me, was simple and fundamental: study. That way, when you stretch your money so it can reach a house that seems outside your budget, you'll be as sure as a person can be that it'll pay off.

"People say, 'You're in Beverly Hills. What else do you need?' Well, as you can see, I need some furniture," he said. It was true—by this time we were sitting in a vast, largely unfurnished living room, which was adjacent to a lovely, but empty, dining room. "Reach for the highest possible house you can. It's going to be a stretch, but your greatest return will come if you reach higher. So, yeah, basically I bought the best value that I could. The furniture—you get a better return on a house than on a dining room set, so I put more into the house. My last vacation was spent at the Doubletree for a hundred dollars a night. Could I fly first class with my family? Yeah, probably. Could I spend four hundred dollars a night on a hotel? Yeah. But what for? I'm a Motel Six guy. I'd rather spend the money here." (I spoke with Weisfeld again a year later, and the first thing he told me was "I got a dining room set!")

Even though he believes that a home is the single best investment a person can make, Weisfeld doesn't advocate large mortgages, which is another way he decreases the uncertainty that's inherent in risk. For him to be comfortable buying a house, he feels he needs to put down more cash up front than most buyers would on the same home.

Our conversation took place well before the subprime mortgage crisis, and Weisfeld sounds even wiser now than when we spoke. "Here's some nuts and bolts for you: you can't spend money that you don't have, right? So this no-money-down stuff—you can't do that. You know what I say? Put as much money down as you possibly can. As *much* as you possibly can. Every penny you have. If you do that, you're coming from a position of power. I put down sixty-five percent on this house. One point seven million. I've got a million-dollar loan. So, there you've got a million-dollar loan on what you expect will one day be a four-million-dollar house. And all you're banking on in this situation is living in the house long enough for it to appreciate. This is what I've always done. I'm not a flipper. I *live* here. I'm nine for nine. I've made money on all nine houses."

Weisfeld's real estate philosophies are risky in the sense that while the array of possible outcomes is narrower than it is for most homebuyers, he's playing with more chips. If his strategies have worked, it is probably due to his obsessive study of home prices. His interest in real estate might have been just that, an interest—the way some people are interested in fantasy football or the early work of Currier and Ives. But his "eye" has in fact been carefully cultivated. "I go to an open house or two every week, and I'm not even looking to move. But I want to see apples to apples at all times. You've got to know what's going on in the market," he said.

This practice—trying to know everything—has served Weisfeld well. In May 2004, he made a profit of $800,000 on a home in Playa del Rey that he had bought for a million dollars four years earlier. That's a ridiculously good return, and you're probably thinking, The lucky bastard. Sure, in that case he was able to ride a historically good real estate market. But he found similar success, before and after, in good and bad markets, which shows the extent to which Weisfeld's studiousness has helped him take risks that turn out well. Having no place to live after cashing out of the Playa del Rey home, Weisfeld moved his family temporarily into a cramped, eight-hundred-square-foot home he had bought as an investment fifteen years earlier, in nearby Mar Vista—another smart risk, as it turns out. He'd paid $250,000 for it in

1990, only to see its value drop to $150,000 after a year. He'd decided to keep it, mostly because he had taken out one of his characteristically diminutive mortgages—25 percent down—and racked up equity quickly. "My wife, who I was dating at the time, said I was crazy," he said. A decade passed before he broke even. But in the four years after that, the home's value tripled, to $750,000. He still has it, it's fully paid off, and he collects $1,800 in rent each month. Free money.

If you're thinking Weisfeld is some sort of real estate savant, he will be the first to tell you he is not. Making the moves he made without also making a prodigious effort to learn about the market would have been reckless. But, fortunately for him, he learned about the value of research early in his adult life, when he bought and sold his first house for a quick profit.

"I was twenty-three," he said. "It was in Venice [California]." Weisfeld and I were leaning against the wrought iron fence surrounding his backyard pool. "I took my dad in with me for the negotiations. They were asking $145,000—this was in 1986. My dad thought I was crazy. I was there with my dad and my best friend. Now, my dad was my role model, my pillar in life, right? I thought he would be really excited. My friend and I offered $150,000, but there were some other offers. So then my friend offered $155,000. The agent said, 'You're going to get this house.' My dad lost it. He cussed me and the realtor out, and he left—he left us to do the negotiations ourselves. He said, 'I didn't teach you to pay full price for anything.' He told the real estate agent she was taking advantage of kids. And he took off. Well, we closed in December of '86 at $155,000. In October of the next year, we sold it for $225,000. And I was on my way. That turned me into a man. I became a man in my dad's eyes."

He also came out wiser than he went in. After that confluence of nerve, determination, and prudence, other people might have thought, Hey, I'm a genius! I have a gift! But Weisfeld knew better. Instead, he thought to himself, Hey, maybe if I do even more *research* and *work* next time, I'll make even more money. It was a lesson that transcended real estate.

He stopped talking for a few seconds (not something he does often) and gripped the iron fence tight, giving it a little shake, and looked around his yard.

"No offense to me, but one would not think that I would be where I am," he said. "If I can do it, it means it can be done."

Calculate Every Risk — Even the One You Live In

"This view — this is my *insurance*."

On a paved, leafy crest overlooking the Austin skyline, I found a guy who looked at real estate risk in much the same way that Weisfeld did: Your primary residence is a huge investment, so make it count. Get the best one you possibly can.

I had driven west of the city, toward Lake Travis. I turned up a hill, arriving at a row of houses that looked back at Austin, over a valley and a reservoir known as Lake Austin, which is actually the dammed-up Colorado River. I was out of breath by the time I reached Steve Wolford's front door, the first one I knocked on in Texas. The house looked new, and, sure enough, Wolford told me that he and his wife had custom built it — all forty-three hundred square feet of it, including the spectacular, cantilevered decks. We talked for a few minutes, Wolford leaning against the door, me on the front steps. He was barefoot and wore khaki shorts and a faded lavender T-shirt. He described the hugeness of the undertaking, building this house. Said the look of it was his wife's doing. It was indeed a lovely place, but I wasn't comprehending its real value. I was missing something. I think Wolford sensed this. And so, once he decided that I was not seeking his religious conversion or trying to sell him anything, he hesitated for a half second and then, smiling as if he couldn't resist, said, "Come here, you've gotta see this."

He waved me inside to show me the view east: the far-off buildings of downtown, the meandering Lake Austin, the valley like a bowl full of trees, the pale, dry Texas sky painted like a wash above everything. Wolford's arms were folded, and he grinned. I just stared, openmouthed.

He waved a hand and said—with pride, it sounded like, and a bit of a drawl—"This view—this is my *in*surance."

Insurance is a good thing, and Wolford was right: someone would always want that view. (Just like Carole Reichhelm from chapter 1 was right that people will always want to live on the water, and Susan Anderson from chapter 2 was right that people will forever want to live in Westport, Connecticut.) General George S. Patton, who always seems to turn up in books like this sooner or later, hinted at this when he said, "Take calculated risks. That is quite different from being rash." Indeed, there's often a fine line between brilliant and bat-shit crazy. An adventurous spirit is wonderful, but not if it makes you do things you can't afford. Wolford seemed to have little problem affording his home—it was well furnished and painstakingly decorated in bright reds and purples, with faux columns flanking the entrance to the dining room and a long black S-shaped sofa by the living room fireplace—but, still, he thought of it as an asset as well as a dwelling. He confided that he sometimes thought about selling it, even though that hadn't been the point of building it. The value had already increased considerably. Nearby, a very, very rich man was building a $57 million home, the kind of thing that tends to give a boost to the neighborhood property values.

Putting up a house this big and expensive was a risk for Wolford, as it would be for many people, but it was a calculated risk. That magnificent Texas vista, as Wolford saw it, was very necessary insurance. I guessed he probably wouldn't have built the same house on the other side of the street, where the only view was of the homes that had great views.

Look for Your Window to Go Solo

"I used to hire consultants myself. I had rewritten enough of their reports to know that I could do it better."

I found another great example of calculated risk in Lake Forest, Illinois, a quiet Chicago suburb where I spent a cloudy Saturday. A friend of mine grew up there, and his parents directed me to a few prime streets — mostly places where they knew people whose stories might fit into this book. Not that the town, number thirty on my top one hundred wealthiest list, had any shortage of people who had done well for themselves. Half the residents earn more than $164,906 each year, and the average home value is $929,715.

I don't know exactly where Ron Irvine falls into the town's impressive wealth statistics, but I do know that he lives in a large, bleached-brick, primly landscaped home on a peaceful cul-de-sac—a house that's above the median, I would guess. When he answered the door, I dropped my friend's folks' names, and Irvine, whose wife was chatting with a guest in the dining room, welcomed me in for a short chat. We sat in the living room, my backside cradled by one of the most comfortable pieces of furniture I can ever recall dropping myself onto. The living room was brightened only by the cottony, overcast light from outside.

Irvine told me he had once been a corporate man, spending his early working years at G.D. Searle, the pharmaceutical company, of which Donald Rumsfeld was then the CEO. By 1987, after Rumsfeld had overseen the company's acquisition by Monsanto and moved on, Irvine had reached a slot in the corporate hierarchy where he could have remained for a long time: director of market planning and research. It was a comfortable job with a good salary, but high enough up the ladder that he felt there wasn't much more room for growth or promotion. "As a thirty-three-year-old African American director, I didn't see a lot of steps ahead of me," he said. "I decided to set my own sails."

He launched Irvine Consulting, Inc., in October of that year. Setting his own sails might have seemed rash — he had two young children and was leaving a secure job — but, in fact, it was a move that Irvine had calculated as precisely as he could. For one thing, at the time, American companies were under increasing pressure by Congress and the culture to hire minority contractors and businesses. Also, Irvine himself had gained a deep knowledge of the pharmaceutical industry, and he had been a part of the process by which Searle and other firms hired consultants in areas such as product development and concept testing. He knew the qualities that corporations sought in these outside contractors. And Irvine knew what he and his colleagues said after the consultants left the room.

"I used to hire consultants myself," he said. "I had rewritten enough of their reports to know that I could do it better." So he became one. When he started his own firm, Irvine wasn't exhibiting *risky* behavior, like deciding that because you're a good cook you're going to throw your kid's college fund into a restaurant (the type of business that fails most often, they say). He already had clients lined up, he knew how to make a pitch to land new ones, and he knew how to do the work. Within four years, Irvine Consulting, Inc., had seven full-time employees and revenues of $2.3 million.

You Want Autonomy? Let It Motivate You

"The question is, If you fail, what could happen? The company tanks, and you go out and get a job. So why not try it?"

The sun flooded Silicon Valley. The northern California wind was blowing my hair into a mess. And the mayor of Atherton, Charles Marsala, told me we were on our way to the home of a man named Rich Miletic, who owned a company that tested equipment for communications networks. When Marsala pulled up in front of Miletic's house in the Ferrari, top down, Miletic was loading his SUV for a ski trip with his wife, Lisa, and their children. He took a break to talk in his living room.

Miletic is quarterback handsome and has a broad smile. He grew up in working-class Chicago. His parents had immigrated to the United States—his father from what would become Yugoslavia, his mother from Germany—after World War II. She worked for AT&T on the 411 telephone information line, and Miletic's dad was a maintenance manager at apartment buildings around the city. Eventually, Rich worked for his father, dumping garbage, cleaning carpets, washing windows. The older Miletic assigned the jobs, but for most of each day, Rich worked alone. "I didn't really have a boss, and I got used to that at a young age," he said.

Miletic went on to earn a degree in engineering from the University of Illinois at Urbana-Champaign, paying the tuition with his summer earnings. He went to graduate school at night at DePaul, earned his MBA, and, after that, took corporate jobs at Honeywell and then Motorola. At those companies he had bosses to report to and co-workers to get along with, which, while not a problem for him—Miletic seemed affable and easygoing to me—caused him to squirm uncomfortably under the constraints of corporate culture. He generally detested the whole working-for-the-Man arrangement.

But doesn't *everybody* hate working for a boss? Even if the boss is a mensch, don't most people wish they could run their own company or work from home in their pajamas? *Be* the boss? Maybe, but simple math tells us that the overwhelming majority of people cannot be and will never be the boss. (Who would work for them?) Still, Miletic sought out positions of autonomy. Not because he had a big ego, but because he felt he was at his best when working independently. He eventually left Motorola for the high-tech company Safco, which tests and improves wireless networks, where he learned of a new opportunity—Safco wanted to set up a sales office in Hong Kong. Miletic had never been to Hong Kong. Or Asia. But he would be the only person in the office, and that sounded good. His hand shot up in the air.

"I took my wife and my laptop and went to Hong Kong," he told me, smirking. "When I got there, I dug up some office space and hired a secretary. I had always had the idea of starting my own company in the back of my mind. So this was, for me, a way to do it with someone behind me, a big company." A risk but a relatively safe risk.

Even though he had the comforting resources of a corporation available to him, Miletic still got to feel like something of an explorer, off on his own in a strange land, setting up an office that would be unlike any post back in the States. He assumed it wouldn't be easy, and it wasn't—and he liked that. "There's no Best Buy where you can just go out and get all your computer equipment. There are all these little mom-and-pop shops that you have to find. We didn't even have a business license, so we couldn't get a bank account at first. It took a few months to get everything set up," he said.

Within two years of his arrival in Hong Kong, the office Miletic had set up was bringing in between $4 million and $5 million in sales—a resounding success. He was the boss of his expatriate fiefdom. But he still wasn't the boss of himself.

"Eventually I got the itch to move on," he said. Through his connections in the communications business, in 1996 he heard about a company called ZK Celltest that was for sale in Silicon Valley. He figured out a way to buy it, leveraging future earnings to minimize the amount of money he would have to post up front. Finally, Rich Miletic was boss. It was a feeling he had tasted back when he used to mow lawns, and when he was setting up the Hong Kong office. But now, for the first time, he answered to no one.

He told me he enjoyed the path he followed to get there because he took risks that were just iffy enough to make them exciting but never so uncertain as to put his or his family's future in jeopardy. He always knew, to the extent that anyone can know, what the potential outcomes were of any decision. If he could live with the worst outcome, he went for it.

When Rich Miletic bought ZK Celltest, he planned to run it for five years and then sell it. "It's been ten," he told me. "You have to take risks, but you have to take calculated risks. If I never did, I'd still be in Chicago working for Motorola. Half the time, when I take a risk or try a new thing, I do it for fun. The question is, If you fail, what could happen? The company tanks, and you go out and get a job. So why not try it? Money is important, but it's not the most important thing."

The key word here is *fun*. For Miletic, autonomy is fun. His desire for independence ran deep. And he had so much fun chasing that independence that he was willing to consider any path that might lead to it. Even the one that led through Hong Kong.

If you were to look at Miletic's résumé, with no annotations or commentary elaborating the various jobs he's had, you would see what looked like a fortunate career, stacked with bold moves and increasingly dramatic job changes. A lucky guy, you might think—his gambles paid off. Or at least a gutsy guy. And it's true: in his career, Miletic has made some risky moves, in that they could have yielded any one of a number of outcomes, not all of which included a home in America's richest ZIP code. But he never took a single flyer on a job that he wasn't completely confident he could handle. He possessed two qualities that all but ensured his success: an openness to trying new things, and the ability to judge which risks were good ones. And as a former editor of mine once pointed out, you've got to possess *both* of those qualities. If you're open to trying new things but you lack judgment, you're more likely to end up sitting around barefoot in Golden Gate Park drinking warm beer and singing Janis Joplin songs than living in Atherton.

Be Cocky When It Counts

"There's only one reason you should give me this deal:
me and my guys — we have fire in our eyes."

So far, the people I've introduced who talked about risk — Heidi Roizen, Jeff Weisfeld, Ron Irvine, Rich Miletic — have treated the subject in an almost academic way: measured, rational, calculated. This is as it should be, and it's why they live where they do.

But I don't want to sell those people short. What they have done requires, for lack of a more couth term, balls. Weisfeld moved his wife and two kids into an eight-hundred-square-foot home for fifteen months after making a whopping $800,000 profit on a million-dollar house. Irvine, with two young children running around the house, left corporate America for an office in his den. Miletic went to Hong Kong. These people showed courage, confidence, and cunning. The risks they took were well calculated, rational, and even fun, but make no mistake: they had guts.

For a more concentrated display of fortitude — the guts of a single moment — I'll turn to one Vivek Ranadivé. You might have heard of him. He wrote a book in 1999 called *The Power of Now,* which became a *New York Times* bestseller. The book explains Ranadivé's theory that the flow of real-time information can dramatically improve a company's business. Ranadivé is the CEO of a company called Tibco, which helps companies speed up the flow of information so that everyone always knows what's happening across the firm, and across the stock market, in real time. His software was revolutionary at the time he brought it to market, and it helped turn Ranadivé into a Silicon Valley legend.

I visited him at the Tibco offices in Palo Alto, which isn't far from Atherton, where Ranadivé lives. My escort, again, was Mayor Charles Marsala, who this time scooted his Ferrari into a parking spot outside one of the many low, new-looking buildings at Tibco's campus-like headquarters.

Marsala and I waited in a conference room for Ranadivé, who was running a few minutes late. We made small talk with a friendly public relations woman from the company, who would be sitting in. It was all very normal until the door opened and in walked Roger Craig, three-time Super Bowl champion and the NFL's Most Valuable Player in 1988. He was enormous and very friendly, and he sat right next to me. No explanation was given for his presence. We made small talk with him too.

Next came a chef. I knew because he was dressed like a chef. He knocked, entered, and asked for our lunch orders. Craig ordered "the Vivek salad," which I assumed to be the boss's favorite. Now, it happened to be Saint Patrick's Day, and I was craving corned beef. My Irish American mother always made corned beef and cabbage on Saint Patrick's Day, so it was the first thing that popped into my head.

"What kind of sandwiches do you have?"

"All kinds," the chef replied.

"All kinds? Really?"

"Try me."

"Corned beef and Swiss on rye, mustard," I challenged.

"Would you like that grilled?"

When Ranadivé arrived, his own Vivek salad (which, as I recall, had a lot of corn in it) already waiting for him, I told him a little about the Mayor Marsala tour—the people I had met, the

Ferrari, Barry Bonds's old house. Silicon Valley was quite a place, I said.

He nodded and smiled. "My son Andre is in high school now," he said. "When he was about seven, he opened a lemonade stand. Before long he had two hundred dollars in a little box. When your ZIP code is 94027, and Larry Ellison [cofounder and CEO of Oracle Corporation] lives two doors down. . . . Now my son has a music business. When my daughter, who is now thirteen, was in fourth grade, she came home from school one day and said she'd learned how to start a company. The area's a bit wacky."

This was a few years after the dot-com proliferation had stopped proliferating, but Ranadivé pointed out the inordinate number of technology influencers who still populated the area. "One of my favorite cities in the world is Florence, and when you go into the church of Santa Croce there, you see all those guys who lived around the same time in that same area," he said, sounding like a retiree reminiscing about a stop on a Tuscan bus tour. But then he added, "That's sort of what this area is like right now." Whoa. Here was a man, not yet fifty, sitting across a conference room table from me, wearing a golf shirt, not touching his salad, casually comparing himself and his neighbors to the men whose remains lie in a church founded, legend has it, by Saint Francis of Assisi himself: Michelangelo, Machiavelli, Galileo, Rossini.

The audacity of his statement didn't hit me until I was typing up my notes that evening, but now as I think about it, of *course* he's audacious. Audacity is what drove Ranadivé, after arriving in the United States in 1975 with, as he says, "fifty dollars in my pocket" and a spot in the freshman class at the Massachusetts Institute of Technology, to build Tibco into a company with a one-time valuation of more than $1 billion. And the people who live in and around Silicon Valley—well, maybe they are geniuses. But instead of monuments in the Basilica of Santa Croce, these guys and their billions of dollars and their innovative companies will be memorialized on the very shrine they helped construct: the Internet.

The "Tib" in Tibco stands for "*the* *i*nformation *b*us." It is Rana-divé's term for what his software does, which is to help companies integrate all their disparate pieces of software and information into one fluid, real-time system. "The power of now," as he calls it. His first earth-moving innovation, famously, was to bring real-time stock quotes and information to the desktop computers of Wall Street firms in the late 1980s. He converted that success into what Tibco is today, and he now serves all kinds of companies, not just investment houses.

What I learned from our conversation, though, didn't have to do with the inner workings of Tibco or the complex software solutions Randivé had developed. It was his story about a moment in 1989, when he was promoting MarketSheet, his stock market information synchronization system. He was eager to net big Wall Street clients—Fidelity had recently signed on, but Salomon Brothers, one of the financial sector's biggest fish, was also interested. Salomon was shopping around for a company to provide the kind of services Ranadivé offered. The bank had narrowed the field, which wasn't wide to begin with, to Ranadivé—"me, this young punk, and my seven guys," as he puts it—and the giant IBM. The two contenders were in the midst of what the investment bank called a bake-off, feverishly jumping through hoops trying to prove that their system was better. In the dead of summer, Ranadivé told me, he flew from San Francisco to New York City to have lunch with the brokerage firm's chief of technology.

Ranadivé and the chief of technology sat in a private, air-conditioned dining room, sealed off from the sticky heat that baked the Wall Street asphalt outside. The chief of technology smoked a cigar that smelled so bad Ranadivé could hardly eat.

Toward the end of the meal, the man finally asked, "Okay, why should I give you this business?"

Ranadivé was expecting this, and he delivered a well-rehearsed answer stating the reasons his company could do the contract. The guy rolled his eyes and cut off Ranadivé.

"Come on, Vivek. Why should I really work with you?"

This jarred the young punk. Ranadivé hesitated, then went into his speech again. The chief of technology blew a big puff of smoke in his face. Ranadivé paused, looked at the floor, and took a deep breath. It was a crucial moment. Maybe he thought about what got him here in the first place: his brilliant idea, his ability to bring it to market. Or maybe he thought about the first day he set foot in America, back in 1975, a stranger from India with fifty bucks and an MIT dorm assignment, and realized how far he had come. Whatever it was, something stirred in him. Shook him. He decided to abandon all talk of numbers and projections and software solutions. He summoned nerve he didn't know he had, and he looked the chief of technology in the eye.

"Okay," Ranadivé said, glaring. "There's only one reason you should give me this deal: me and my guys, we have fire in our eyes."

After a long, tense moment, the chief of technology smiled. Ranadivé won the contract.

As he told me this story, Ranadivé threw off an intensity that you rarely feel from people you just met. His thin fingers were interlaced in front of him. He still hadn't touched his salad. He was making a point. Like his illustrious contemporaries in "wacky" Silicon Valley, Ranadivé was telling me that he knows how and when to put himself on the line. When he told the man about the fire in his eyes, that was a risk. What if the guy was looking for a completely different answer? Numbers, projections, efficiency targets? But it was the gut truth, the only thing Ranadivé knew in his bones. When he takes a risk, he does it with every ounce of confidence and insurance he can muster. (Even when coaching his daughter's basketball team. "I never played basketball in my life, but my daughter started playing last year," Ranadivé told me, as I finished my corned beef sandwich. "So I found a young lady who had been an All-American basketball player in college, whose last name happens to be Craig"—Roger Craig, who I later found out was Tibco's director of business development, cracked up at this— "and asked her to be my assistant coach. I would do a full-court press right away, every game, and we'd be up twenty-five to nothing in the first quarter.")

Ranadivé and I shook hands before he left the room. A waiter was about to take away his salad, which still sat untouched. He hadn't had one bite. I offered to eat it if it was going to be thrown away.

What I learned from Ranadivé was don't pretend. Don't try to give the right answer. In the business world, in negotiations, in job interviews—in none of these situations should you tamp down what's in your heart. You've wanted to work at Company XYZ since you were nine? Maybe you ought to say so. You want to head up a big project to land a new client? Step up and make your case, because no one's going to make it for you. You think you deserve someone's business because of the lava in your belly and the fire in your eyes? Say it. It worked for Vivek Ranadivé. Dude's got his own salad.

Don't Worry about What Other People Think

"You have to be willing to break some glass once in a while."

Not many people, I guess, are as gutsy as Ranadivé was in that moment at Salomon Brothers. Oh, enough are, of course — without them, there would be fewer mergers, acquisitions, sudden firings, unlikely hires, blown deals, secret meetings, and blockbuster transactions. But for every instance of conspicuous gumption, there are thousands of workers who plod along in their jobs, doing what they're told, complacent and unimaginative. Which is why anyone who bends the rules even a little bit can go far.

In the large, open kitchen of a Tudor house the size of a small high school, an oil painting hung over a fireplace that was big enough to roast a boar in. The owner of the painting (and of the house) related to me its plot: A young boy had apparently thrown a rock, shattering a shop window, which was visible in the background on the right side of the painting. In the foreground, the shopkeeper clutched another boy by the collar, scolding him for committing the crime. Off to the left, in the shadow of a tree, the real culprit snickered.

"He's got the wrong guy," said my host, a sixty-nine-year-old businessman named Joseph Gorman. I was in Cleveland — or, rather, in the suburb of Gates Mills, number ninety-six on the top hundred wealthiest, one town beyond the more well-known haven of Shaker Heights. In Gates Mills, fewer homes are scattered over the acreage than in Shaker Heights, and before long I found myself standing at the stone gate marking the entrance to Moxahela Farm, a corner of churned, brown earth at a sleepy suburban crossroads, where Gorman lived. (By the time I actually reached his front door, I had enjoyed lengthy visits with the residents of two other homes on his property. See chapter 5 for the stories of the other folks I met at Moxahela.)

Gorman, the affable multimillionaire standing next to me in front of the gaping fireplace, was chuckling about how the other kid in the painting got away with throwing the rock. I liked Gorman from the moment he opened the thick wood door to his home. But I almost didn't meet him. I really, *really* wanted someone to be home at this place—I only had one full day in Cleveland, and I had spent a fruitless hour pacing quiet roads caked with dry winter sand—but a caretaker on the property had told me he wasn't sure anyone was around. I stood on Gorman's Tudor stoop for an extra-long time, glancing around, peeking in windows, a serf at the steps of the lord. I assume I was being filmed by multiple security cameras as I stood desperately trying to hear the telltale muted thuds of feet on the way to the door.

I had already turned to leave when the door latch clicked and a quick rush of air sucked into the house. Gorman stood tall, even in tube-socked feet. His sandy hair matched his gold-rimmed glasses, and he wore gray shorts and a gray Thomas M. Cooley Law School T-shirt. He had just finished his workout, he told me. He looked at me, friendly but a little wary. I told him what I was doing, and he smiled and nodded a little, as if to say, Okay, could be interesting. He invited me in for a quick chat—he had to get ready for a big charity function his wife was orchestrating downtown that evening. We stood on the marble floor of his sky-high atrium foyer, which opened up to the balconied second floor.

Wood paneling shellacked every conceivable surface, grandfather clocks ticked in more than one corner, and oil paintings in gilded frames decorated the long walls. I looked around for the museum gift shop.

As we talked, Gorman led me on a tour of his art collection, which took us through several rooms on the multitiered first floor of the house, built in 1900. Favorites in his collection are a pair of paintings of monkeys by the English artist George Lance. "Churchill only had one painting in his World War One bunker, and it was a Lance monkey painting," Gorman said. He was no casual collector, that much was clear.

Gorman was a company man, but one different from most — different from the guy who works for thirty-five years, never screwing up too bad, never knocking anyone's socks off, and retires with a gold watch and a pension. That would not have satisfied Gorman, because he was too curious (curiosity being one of the defining features of risk takers). After graduating from Yale Law School and spending a few years as a general corporate counsel, at age thirty he joined the legal department of TRW, Inc., a technology-based corporation in the automotive safety and aerospace fields. The space and defense components have since been sold to other companies, but the automotive division still employs more than sixty-six thousand people and posted sales of $14.7 billion in 2007. (The Robert Lindsey book *The Falcon and the Snowman*, and the movie by the same name starring Sean Penn, told the true story of two friends, one a drug dealer and the other an employee for TRW — which at the time was a government defense contractor assisting in spy satellites — who sold secrets to the Soviets. In the movie, TRW is called RTX.)

Elevating himself from the legal department to the offices of chairman and chief executive officer, positions he held for fourteen years, required a fair amount of playing by the rules over the decades Gorman spent at TRW. But in fact it was his occasional bending of unwritten corporate rules that propelled him past his colleagues. "You have to be willing to break some glass once in a while," he told me, his voice coming down hard on the word *glass*. "Now, if all your boss ever hears is the roaring crash and din of shattering glass, that's maybe too much. But when the occasion and opportunity are right, you've *got* to do it."

I asked Gorman what he meant by breaking some glass, and he thought about it for a moment, rubbing his eyes. "When I was general counsel for TRW, we used to do these three hundred and sixty–degree reviews that were anonymous," he said. "Everyone above and below you gives some feedback about you. When I went in for mine, they sat me down and said, 'People really like you, but they say you're always trying to do everyone else's job. You want to do the finance job, the human resources job, and every other person's job, and people think you should just stay out of it and do your own job.'" Gorman paused, smiling as mischievously as the kid in the painting who had broken the window. "And then they said, 'But we'd like you to keep doing what you're doing.' And eventually they bumped me upstairs, so I guess it worked."

To his bosses, Gorman's nosing around in other people's work showed an admirable interest in the greater success of TRW outside of the legal department, but it was also risky business. It could have turned Gorman's co-workers against him (and it sounds like a few of them did turn). Had Gorman been working for less enlightened bosses, his meddling could have backfired. But instead of a busybody, the higher-ups saw a bright young man whose talents would be wasted if he was confined to the duties of a general counsel. "I just always believed that you have to know more than anyone else in the room on any subject," he said. So they let him see what influence he could have on other parts of the company until he wound up running the whole thing.

During his career, Gorman had flown to foreign countries with dignitaries (he accompanied the first President Bush on the trip to Japan during which the president famously vomited during dinner), advised President Clinton on foreign trade, and headed the United States–Japan Business Council. "I've had an interesting, colorful, fun career," he said. By now, he could very well be retired, enjoying his thirty acres and three hundred fruit trees, traveling, serving on a board here and there. But where's the fun in that? Where's the risk? A few years back, Gorman founded Moxahela Enterprises—*moxahela,* the name of his farm, is Iroquois for "bear gorge"—a firm that invests in very-early-stage start-up companies. He calls it a "venture catalyst."

"We just invested in a new company that stores energy in the form of ice. [Check out www.ice-energy.com.] And that's just one of twenty-four things or companies I'm interested in right now. Another is Snow Aviation. They're rebuilding and retrofitting C-one-thirty planes to accommodate the shorter takeoff and landing strips in the Middle East and to fit Stryker armored tanks—the cargo doors weren't wide enough to fit the tanks on the planes," he said. Gorman understands the value he brings to these start-ups, and it extends beyond the obvious financial backing. "Most early-stage companies fail not because of a lack of funding but because of a lack of knowledge and a lack of experience." Both of which he has in abundance.

Obviously, Gorman is in good enough financial shape to be able to enter a field as uncertain as high-risk venture capital, which must remove some of the anxiety. But there is high risk nonetheless — it's not like he wants to throw money away — and the risk seems to be what he's in it for. I gathered that he was after the thrill of discovering a new business, and if he had to break a little glass to find it, so be it. "This isn't retirement. I wouldn't call it that," he said. "And very little of what I do right now is about money."

I had heard that same sentiment back in Atherton, California, expressed by Silicon Valley real estate developer Dave Dollinger. "It doesn't matter how much money you have. All the people I know who have a lot of money are still working," Dollinger had said. "I don't go out and do another real estate deal right now because I want to make a dollar. I do it because it's fun, and I like putting deals together."

What happened, though, was that Dollinger — and Joseph Gorman, Vivek Ranadivé, and Rich Miletic — made money despite themselves. They may be driven by some force other than the desire for more dollars, but that drive just so happens to generate wealth as well as satisfaction. After meeting and talking with these people and asking them what really moves them, what gets them out of bed every morning, I believe it's not financial gain but simple satisfaction. Their hunger for the feeling that comes when a risk pays off — a big raise, a big promotion, a pat on the back, a new job, more responsibility, more work but *better* work — is never sated. When you accomplish one of these goals, you feel joy. Some relief too. The adrenaline starts pumping, so you feel some physical excitement. You feel good. You feel smart.

These stories made me think of Ben Cohen, a famous example of an obscenely wealthy businessman who was driven by the thrill of a smart, principled risk, not by money. In 1978 Cohen started a homemade ice cream shop at an abandoned gas station in Burlington, Vermont, with his friend Jerry Greenfield. They called their ice cream Ben & Jerry's, and its story is chronicled in the spirited book, *Ben & Jerry's: The Inside Scoop,* by Fred "Chico" Lager, the company's former CEO. (I met Jerry once at a store-opening in Vermont. We actually shared a sundae.)

The company grew quickly, from $135,000 in revenue in 1980 to $1.5 million in 1983. They needed a larger factory, which would require $700,000 in capital. The company was still run like a local business, and it faced the prospect of having to sell out to venture capitalists or go public, which would entail time-consuming and expensive filings with the U.S. Securities and Exchange Commission, including the kind of audited financial records Ben and Jerry did not have.

Ben had an idea: What about a public stock offering that was only available to residents of Vermont? After all, back when the two friends were scooping ice cream as fast as they could make it, at the old gas station, loyal Vermonters had stood in line to wait for it. Why not let them in on the action instead of Wall Street? And why not lower the minimum buy in, typically in the thousands of dollars for an initial public offering, to a hundred bucks or so? "The object of the in-state offering is to allow the average Vermonter the opportunity to invest in and hopefully profit from Ben & Jerry's—an ice cream company which the average Vermonter supported, made famous, and allowed to prosper," Cohen wrote in a memo. "The premise is that the small Vermont investor should have the same opportunity to profit as the large venture capitalist."

Cohen was all but laughed at by almost every bank and lawyer in the state. But he finally found a lawyer who would help him, and they eventually found a bank to underwrite the offering. If the offering didn't end up raising enough money, Ben & Jerry's would have to return every penny to anyone who invested and then seek alternate funding. They'd also have to postpone construction of the new factory, keeping their production line from meeting demand in the coming year, which would mean flat or negative sales growth.

A crazy risk? Not to Cohen. He didn't care what the experts said. He *knew* Vermonters. He knew in his heart that they would jump at the chance to own a piece of one of the largest, most well-known companies in the state, a company that supported local dairy farmers and gave money back to the community. He had faith, and that faith was based on something real, something he had witnessed. It removed some of the tension from the risk.

Cohen had so much faith that he set the time period that the stocks would be offered at one month, an unusually short period in which to sell 73,500 shares. Cohen himself traversed the state for weeks, holding informational meetings in hotel conference rooms, scooping ice cream, and telling locals about the plan.

In the end, every last share was sold. One in every hundred state households bought stock, and about a third of the buyers purchased the minimum amount: twelve shares for $126. Today, you can take a tour of the sprawling factory in Waterbury—bought and paid for largely by Vermont residents—and taste ice cream fresh off the line.

Would a man who cared only about bringing in cash—and who cared what everyone else thought and who was afraid to break a little glass—have done it the way Cohen did?

Reduce Risk by Believing in Yourself

....

**"If they like the clothes I design,
that should be enough to keep them coming back."**

....

A risk doesn't have to be an isolated move—selling a building or buying stock. Risk may be the way you approach your entire business. An attitude of risk often gestates over time as a person grows more confident in his or her work. That was true for the late fashion designer Philip Hulitar, whose casually elegant widow, Mary, I met on a beautiful day in Palm Beach.

It was only noon, but already the sun had baked Palm Beach, a slim breadstick of Florida earth, to a temperature of over ninety degrees. When Mrs. Hulitar opened the door, a blessed breath of the coolness inside puffed out. She had been slicing a mango to have with her lunch, she said, as a way of apologizing for taking so long to answer. We chatted at the door, and she told me a little about her husband, glowing as she spoke of him. A few times she said that she just couldn't invite me in. Too much to do. Eventually, however, perhaps convinced that I really was a writer working on a book and not some huckster, she opened the door wider and waved me inside.

Her husband was a revered fashion designer in the mid-twentieth century, and his style—colorful, bright, clashy—splashed over every room of the house. Despite the movie-set decor, the home was comfortable, the kind of place where you could put your feet up and read or sit on the floor eating cereal. Outside giant windows and across a green lawn, the Atlantic Ocean rolled onto the Hulitars' private beach.

Up a short set of stairs from the front door, a long hall that was once an open breezeway led to the main living area. Its walls were covered with yellow grass cloth, and on the marble tile floor, a yellow and blue trompe l'oeil carpet of painted canvas stretched like a tongue past the swimming pool, past the kitchen, and into a great room with an ocean view. As we passed the kitchen, where the mango sat half cut, I heard the Saturday broadcast of the Metropolitan Opera.

Hulitar is a diminutive woman with pale eyes the color of water on nautical charts, and she wore a frayed blue oxford shirt, white cotton pants, and crisp New Balance sneakers. She told me she had given up smoking three years before, and I could hear its remnant rasp in her voice. We sat and chatted in two bright yellow armchairs in a room with a full wall of books, a cluttered desk, paintings of her two daughters on another wall, and a view of the water. Decades of feet resting on the floor had worn rough patches into the carpet in front of each chair.

Philip Hulitar was the chief designer for Bergdorf Goodman, the high-fashion department store on Fifth Avenue in New York City. He specialized in cocktail dresses and evening gowns, and Mary often wore clothes he had dreamed up. ("That was as far as I got involved in the business—wearing the dresses," she said.) Philip had tried out a career on Wall Street, hated it, and began designing clothing instead.

After making a name for himself at Bergdorf, Philip started his own line in 1949. Vintage clothing collectors today covet his dresses. One dealer, Vintage Textile, selling a strapless Hulitar dress and bolero, wrote in the caption on its Web site, "In the end, Hulitar created what matters most in fashion: beauty." Another dealer, Enoki World, writes that his "style ran more toward bombshell than any other label of the day. His hourglass dresses were knockout glamorous for women who already had serious curves and wanted to emphasize them." His obituary in the *New York Times* noted that his designs were featured in the 1958 World's Fair in Brussels. By that time, he had developed enough confidence in his work to adopt an attitude of airy independence, borne of the knowledge that he was a damn good designer. Mary told me that he prided himself on never sending a case of champagne to his buyers around the holidays, as was the custom of many suppliers. "If they like the clothes I design, that should be enough to keep them coming back," he would say.

Judging by this and the way Mrs. Hulitar spoke of her husband—and from the florid, colorful, even flamboyant decoration of his home—he was singularly confident, irrepressible, and didn't much care what the world thought. The logo for his line of dresses and gowns was his name preceded by a small star.

The lesson here is not that you should always be arrogant but that cockiness is better than wimpiness. Less confident designers might have constantly strained to keep buyers happy by sweetening deals with gifts. In much of the fashion industry, this is the norm—air kisses and presents are important parts of its mechanics. But Hulitar didn't feel the need to try to enhance his reputation with frippery. He had broken away from one of the most important names in the fashion world, Bergdorf, and knew he needed to assert himself. Diluting your personality because that's the norm is a slippery slope, and he knew his product and his service were good enough to stand on their own.

When You Fail Miserably, Rejoice

"We came out the stronger for it. I'm a survivor."

Sometimes you hear about a person who makes a drastic change midcareer—someone who applies to law school at age thirty-seven, perhaps, or who somehow goes from a steady gig as an anonymous middle manager to a new life running, say, a successful chain of movie theaters. Sometimes those changes are the result of circumstance. Simple cause and effect. You lose a job or get a divorce, and then you meet a guy who knows a guy who's looking for someone like you, and you need a job, so you decide to take a flyer on the movie theater business. And just like that, you enter a great, new, completely different career. Whether or not it was the plan all along doesn't matter, and whether or not it was trouble that led you to it doesn't matter. What matters is that you found a good new gig.

The significance of these job-jumpers is that they (or at least the ones I met) all found themselves in the same spot: up against the wall. And being up against the wall can be a wonderful thing. A blessing, even. For some people, reaching that point is the only way for them to scratch into their true desires, the only way they're ever going to say, "The hell with it! I want to be a woodworker!" If the company you sweat and toil for goes belly-up or if a big investment tanks or if your personal life gets scrambled up, you might feel a little desperate. That's okay. That can be *good*. You hope the feeling doesn't last, but some people, the smart people, *use* that feeling. They grab hold of their situation and wring it, twisting it in their fists until a drop comes out of it, and that drop tastes like the future. And hell if it's not the most refreshing thing they've ever tasted. A lot better than the bland, anonymous flavor of *middle manager*.

In chapter 1, I mentioned the work of Carol Dweck, a psychologist at Stanford University who sees two kinds of people: those with fixed mind-sets and those with growth mind-sets. A person who loses her job unexpectedly and through no fault of her own had better learn to become the kind of person who can see opportunity where others see squat. That's called a growth mind-set. But if you don't find yourself waltzing through life spotting groundbreaking business opportunities at every turn, don't beat yourself up. Most people don't. A lot of brilliant ideas spring up from the worst of situations, like wonderful children from bad marriages. Desperation, adversity, and uncertainty have a way of stimulating the cleverness and resourcefulness trapped inside people's minds and of teaching them skills they didn't know they had.

Dweck tells the story of George Danzig, a graduate student in mathematics at the University of California, Berkeley, around 1940. During his first year, he arrived late to class one day and quickly jotted down two math problems that were written on the blackboard, assuming they were that evening's homework. A few days passed before he handed them in to the professor, having worked feverishly to solve them, apologizing for being late with the assignment. But the problems he had solved turned out not to be homework. They were, in fact, two famous math problems that had never been solved before.

I met a guy named Jerry Turbett at a bar in Paradise Valley, Arizona, who might not have been a George Danzig, but he certainly found success the hard way. I got to talking to Turbett on a Friday evening at El Chorro's, a clubby bar with a dirt parking lot, where I had met Harland Young, the artist in chapter 3. I stood against the wall with a scotch in my hand, and Turbett walked up and asked about the notebook in the other. He was tall and ruddy, and he introduced me to a few people. Turbett told me he used to sell high-tech equipment, living the salesman's life behind the wheel and flying coach, before he and his now-ex-wife sunk $400,000 of their savings into a start-up fast-food pizza chain. "It was take-home-and-bake pizza," he said, his voice lifting at the end, like a faint grace note of lingering hope for the idea. "If they had managed it right, I think it would have been a winner. But we lost our eggs on that one."

It didn't bankrupt him, not even close. But the loss certainly set him back—and gave him pause. He retreated to his garage, his haven, where he often did woodworking as a hobby. Got his mind off the pizza chain. He worked and worked at his hobby, until one day he realized he could make some money doing this thing he loved.

"That's all over now," he said of the failed pizza shop and marriage. "We came out the stronger for it. I'm a survivor. I'm frugal in some ways, but I've poured every cent I've had into the woodworking shop."

Really? Every cent? Was that wise, in light of that $400,000 loss last time around?

Turbett gave his head a little shake, as if to say, No, there's something you don't understand. This time, it wasn't do-it-yourself pizza. "I'm having the time of my life," he said. "And doing custom cabinetry is like holding up a bank. I just did a stereo cabinet for Tyson Nash, the hockey player for the Coyotes. I feel guilty charging what I do, but people would pay more to get it from a factory."

How strong were the forces of adversity beating down Turbett after the pizza ordeal? I can't say for sure. Happy hour at El

Chorro's was a poor setting for a deep, soul-searching conversation. But he couldn't have been feeling too great when it happened. At the very least, he had become the kind of person who takes (another) big risk, this time on opening a woodworking business out of his garage, which he might not have done were it not for that pizza-store debacle. Thank goodness for that.

If You Hate Your Career, Um, Change It

**"I spent a lot of years in that job,
and I look back on that as a huge strategic error."**

Richard Sander's home was a beautiful structure clad in weathered shingles and wouldn't have looked out of place on a picturesque dirt road on Nantucket. Through a window near the door I saw him amble down the stairs wearing a red-and-black plaid lumberjack shirt. He was hale and sturdy as a log cabin, his hair going chalky white. On this drizzly Friday afternoon in Seattle, he stepped out onto his front step to talk, pulling the door mostly closed behind him.

Sander's father was a local businessman, he told me, focused primarily on a few restaurants that he owned in Seattle. Sander himself became an executive in the airline business, which gave him a front row seat to the hard times that hit Seattle in the 1970s. "At one time there was a billboard out near Sea-Tac, as you leave the city, that said, 'Will the last person to leave Seattle please turn out the lights,' " Sander told me. By 1985, Sander had worked in the industry for eighteen years, rising to become the vice president of marketing at an airline. It paid well, and he had managed to thrive during uncertain times in a traditionally unsteady business, but he wasn't truly happy. He wasn't even a little bit happy.

"I had studied business and transportation, and I thought it would be great," he said of his airline career, pursing his lips and shrugging. "I spent a lot of years in that job, and I look back on that as a huge strategic error."

The airline industry is risky, sure, but at least Sander was established. That wasn't enough, though. He felt a pull toward the business of building houses—arguably, an even less stable vocation. What drove him to take such a big financial and career risk? "Stress," he said. "Half of those years with the airline, I felt like my job was on the line. That's a long time to feel that way." A lot of people feel stressed out by their jobs, but Sander was proof that you could do something about it. "Luckily," he said, "I eventually found a niche."

He walked away from his vice president's office and never looked back. He built the house we were standing in front of, ridding the lot of what he says was a dreary 1950s ranch house. His home looked handsome and well constructed—the man obviously cared about his work. He contrasted his second career to his first, which he had left more than two decades before, and you could still hear the sense of liberation in his voice. "As a real estate developer, you have to have vision. Most people look only at the hassles that go along with developing a property. The key qualities you've got to have are to be a risk taker—but only after doing your due diligence—and to have vision, persistence, and perseverance," he said, adding that his net worth was higher now than it ever would have been had he remained at the airline.

Sander was leaning against a column by the front door. After a moment, I guess he decided we had talked long enough for him to trust me. He turned around, kneed the door open, and said,

"I've got to get going, but first, come on in. You've got to see the view." Outside everything looked dull in the Seattle mist, the color of pavement. But inside Sander's living room, the glow was like whiskey. Through a bay window, the glassy gray waters of Lake Washington spread out beneath the fog that hung over Medina, on the opposite side of the lake, and the Cascades soared above the clouds to the east. I pressed him a little about exactly how you know when it's time to pull the trigger and quit your job — how you know when you're ready to pack up your desk. He talked more about the buildup of stress that led to his fleeing the airline business. Then he sighed, paused, smiled for just a second, and said, "You just know."

Sometimes the Biggest Risk Is Doing Nothing

"My husband had a big offer to take over a company in California, near San Francisco. But I said, 'Not on your life.' "

The word *risk* suggests action. Buy the house. Take the job. Quit the job. Invest in the speculative. Move to Hong Kong. Sometimes, though, the hemming and hawing and researching culminates in a decision to do nothing. To wait. To stay put. And staying put can feel like a very big risk too.

After leaving Sander's, I stopped at a rambling Seattle house that also overlooked Lake Washington, a bit higher up the hill. It was on a short, wavy road that was almost anachronistic in its rusticity. It seemed hidden from the adjacent suburban grid, accessible through a tree-darkened allée that swooped and rose with the topography. A little roof protected the home's front door. The familiar Seattle mist had thickened to a real rain, so this was a good place to stand and knock. The house was wedged into the hillside so as to command the most astounding view possible of water and mountains, which made its shape and design odd. Facing the front door, there was a roof over a lower floor to my right, and I could have almost reached out and touched a window on the floor above. After I rang the doorbell, a hand cranked that upper window open, and a woman's face peeked out.

"Yes?"

I explained myself, and she said okay, she would come down and let me in. First she looked up at the sky and observed, "It's raining."

Marilyn Fite and I sat at an oval wooden table and looked out a window through a thicket of indoor plants. She wore jeans, slippers, and a green sweatshirt that read "Nordland General Store, Marrowstone Island," a local vacation spot. She had reddish, beauty-parlor hair and clutched a tissue as she talked about the ways Seattle had changed over the years, especially since Microsoft and the technology revolution had washed over the city and altered it forever. "We were married in 1955, and we rented a duplex just up the hill from here. Maybe a year later we bought a three-story colonial for sixteen thousand dollars. It just sold for a million," she said, eyebrows raised.

Like many people who have lived in just one place all their lives, Fite seemed to like it better the way it used to be. "In the old Seattle, people didn't talk about their money and wear designer clothes. They were old-shoe people," she said. "This house is getting too big for us. These young people building huge houses—it's too much too soon. Rob Glaser [the uberwealthy founder of RealNetworks] is building down below us here. He just bought *three* pieces of property, all next to each other. Microsoft made a lot of people a lot of money overnight. Bill Gates, sure, I knew his mother, and we know his father very well. She was the head of the United Way here. I was in the Junior League with her. She always said you should give five percent of your income to charity—if you can. She was a great lady. Those kids have good values. I doubt [Bill and Melinda Gates] give their kids supercrazy toys. They're just not that kind of people. But these days everybody wants everything, and they want it faster. And they want a big house, and they want a big car. I mean, I don't even have a cell phone. I see women at the grocery store with cell phones glued to their ears."

Fite declined to go into what line of work her husband, Bartow, was in, but she described him as a hard worker. I asked her about the most momentous decision they had ever made as a couple. She thought for a moment and then said, "Staying in Seattle. My husband had a big offer to take over a company in California, near San Francisco. But I said, 'Not on your life.' We have family here, and friends." Still, it was a big company and the move could have given the Fites a big financial boost. And maybe today they would be richer than they are. But even if they had taken what would have been a sizable risk and moved to California, she didn't think they would have been happier. So they risked even more by staying put. "The American dream is that everybody wants a house with a yard and a chicken in the pot and a new car or whatever. I don't think all that money makes people happy. My mother-in-law said, 'The more you get, the more you have to worry about.' I love to give money away. It drives my husband crazy. The Nature Conservancy, the Trust for Public Land, the Snow Leopard Trust. But we were lucky—we bought a house in the right place at the right time. We were lucky like the people in the computer world were lucky."

Too many people pursuing that American dream jump at every chance that comes along. John D. Rockefeller Jr. once wrote that "every opportunity [implies] an obligation," but that doesn't necessarily mean an obligation to take action. Your obligation is to *consider* every opportunity, to roll it around in your brain, to compare taking it to leaving it. Some opportunities require more mulling than others. Some you can dismiss pretty quickly. You can do that old trick of making a list of the pros and the cons — just writing that here sounds silly, but damn if it doesn't work every time.

The day after I arrived home from Seattle, I received a card in the mail from Marilyn Fite. On the front was a snow leopard. Inside, in neat, ballpoint cursive that reminded me of my grandmother's, she had written a note that shed more light on the way she and her husband had managed their lives. I had walked away admiring their wisdom in rejecting change for its own sake, but her note reminded me that even though they didn't make the Big Move, they also didn't end up with a house overlooking Lake Washington by clipping coupons. She wrote:

> After you left this afternoon I realized (as I was washing my hair) that probably the most important answer to your question is "<u>Be willing to take a chance!</u>"
>
> When I think back over the 60 years we have been married, I remembered the many times my husband was willing to take that chance or, you might say, opportunity! Some worked and some didn't (how to turn your hair gray), but he did it and when you have a wife and 3 young children, plus the assorted beasties, to support, you better not have a weak stomach.

There are many kinds of risks. Little risks, reckless risks, all-or-nothing risks, safe risks. All the risk takers I met, self-described and otherwise, took smart risks. They studied before they acted. Studied the real estate market, studied the consulting business, studied the look in a man's face as he blew cigar smoke, or—most important—studied themselves. Jeff Weisfeld, the Beverly Hills produce broker at the beginning of this chapter, summed up the attitude with a statement that could be applied, metaphorically, to everyone else you just read about: "I go to an open house or two every week, and my house isn't even on the market." He was talking about real estate, of course, not life, but that habit could apply to anything. No matter what your game is, the more you know about a business, the market, and yourself, the bigger the risks you'll be able to take—and the safer you'll feel taking them. So go to the open house. Even if your house isn't on the market.

FIVE

HUMILITY

The Secret Ingredient

All of the people I interviewed for this book were proud of their accomplishments—and rightfully so. It's probably why they talked to me in the first place—my basic question, after all, was, What did you do right? But, in most cases, their pride was small and hard to notice. Some of them smiled sheepishly when I pressed them about the good decisions they had made. Many of them downplayed their success. Most were not proud people by nature. They were simply pleased and felt fortunate that their work and planning had set them up in a dream house and with financial security. As a matter of fact, a lot of them were downright humble—which, as the seven people in this final chapter demonstrate most clearly, is essential to getting ahead.

Howard Stern, the radio personality, has branded himself the

King of All Media, which would seem to suggest brashness, arrogance, and the crassest kind of pride. And he probably has all of those qualities. But the relentless and wildly wealthy Stern also appears to be motivated by an inability to dwell on his own success. In an interview with *Esquire* in 2005 he said, "Whatever I've done at this point doesn't matter. Twenty thousand people show up for a book signing. I sign every book, and afterward I get thoroughly depressed: Oh, my God, what am I going to do next? Honestly, I couldn't even enjoy the moment. It's a sickness. But it keeps me young, man."

That outlook is a form of humility. Stern didn't walk away from that book signing thinking he was Elvis. Humility is one of the essential and surprising ingredients of success. Humility doesn't mean downplaying your abilities or aw-shucksing your way through life. You can swagger and be humble at the same time. Humility makes it okay to roll up your sleeves, stay late when no one else does, and make your own coffee instead of having an assistant do it. Humility makes you work harder.

Never Let Pride Get in the Way of Profit

"I move eighty million dollars a year in produce,
but you're only as good as your last load."

The phone rang in my hotel room in Beverly Hills, and it was a man named Ted Kaplan. He was a friend of a friend, a self-made man, and we had tried unsuccessfully to arrange a meeting while I was in town. But, generously, he offered a few minutes of his time to talk. He spoke mostly about humility — if not overtly.

"When you can write a check for five hundred thousand dollars, you can tell people 'Fuck you,' " he said.

Okay. Let me explain my use of the word *humility* as it applied to Kaplan. He owns a company called Professional Produce, in Los Angeles, a distributor of fruits and vegetables. As a kid he had worked for his father's business, Kaplan Fruit & Produce, lifting boxes and loading trucks. Sweating. Earning every penny of his ten dollars an hour. He learned that no one, not even his father, gives away money for nothing. That fairly obvious realization led him to a deeper, less apparent bit of knowledge: Complacency does not lead to success. No one ever got rich — or, more to the point, stayed rich — by being satisfied.

"I move eighty million dollars a year in produce, but you're only as good as your last load," he said. It sounded as if he was talking while driving a convertible. "I just shipped a load of tomatoes this morning, and that's the last good thing I did. That's all that matters." He added, "The only thing that's kept me alive was knowing how to work hard."

Kaplan is a fast talker, and he's brash, but somehow he's humble too. He understands that the only thing that got him the house in Beverly Hills (he is one of the few people in this book whose home I never saw, but our mutual friend told me it's amazing) was the attitude that he is not the king of the world. That might seem silly to point out, but we've all seen people make a lot of money quickly, convince themselves that everything they touch will turn into a Maserati, stop working as hard as they once did, and end up worse off than they were before the money. (Remember MC Hammer?)

"I may not be the smartest motherfucker around, but I can work harder than anybody. I've got a friend whose great grandmother built the Beverly Hills Hotel. He was born on third base and thinks he hit a triple," Kaplan said. "He's a member of the lucky sperm club."

In other words, work hard.

Well, of course. Everyone knows that. Almost everyone I interviewed uttered those two words within their first few sentences. *Work hard.* As person after person shared that bit of advice, at first I thought: *Come on. Give me something better than that. That sounds like a Boy Scout saying. Pabulum.* But Kaplan made me realize something else: To *want* to work hard, to be willing to sweat, to be willing to get down on your hands and knees and gather the grapefruits that have tumbled out of the crate, your ass crack peeking out above your jeans, your family waiting for you at home . . . well, you *have to* be humble. You must never think you've made it. You must never think you are doing a perfect job or, worse, that your job is done. Because the minute you do, you will lose a little bit of your drive. And if each dollar you earn saps a dollar's worth of drive, eventually, you'll have zero earning power.

A humble person never believes he knows everything or has done everything, and that's what keeps him working hard. He believes there is always more he can learn, that he can always do a better job next time, and that hard work is just part of getting better. The person who isn't humble eventually tapers off, working less and less and less, riding some ever-fading success of the past.

Carol Dweck, the Stanford psychologist, recently developed an experiment to measure people's desire to learn and improve. She gave a test to a series of people—a very difficult test that required clever, strategic responses. After taking the test, each person was shown a computer screen covered with icons, each of which represented someone else who had taken the test. The icons showed the test scores, and by clicking on an icon, you could see what methods and strategies the person had used to answer the same questions. Some people only clicked on icons showing a score lower than their own. They checked the lower scorers' techniques and said later that they walked away feeling better about themselves than when they started because they were smarter than those other people. These people, Dweck told me, believe they were born with a certain amount of intelligence and must constantly prove to themselves and others that it is sufficient. Meanwhile, other participants only checked the icons of test takers who had scored *higher* than they did, with the hope of learning from others who had done better. These participants also walked away with higher self-esteem than when they had begun, but their feeling of heightened self-worth came from the fact that they had *improved* their intelligence, not *validated* it. There's a big difference.

"The people with the fixed mind-sets, at the end of it, said, 'I now feel really good about my abilities, I'm really on top of this subject matter, and I really bolstered my fixed abilities by looking at people who are morons,' " Dweck said. "But the people with growth mind-sets said, 'Intelligence is an ability that can be acquired, so I've got to shore up my acquirable ability. And I can do that by learning.' "

Dweck believes that when success comes, it's perfectly okay to feel good about your achievements, but it's important not to let them define you. "I think it's very normal to be proud of what you've accomplished, and what you've got and how you've enjoyed it," she said. "It's normal to say you feel you have the most beautiful house on the block. But the danger of thinking that you're a god is that you'll stop doing what made you successful."

Be Humble Even If You're As Rich As Brooke Astor

"To spend is easy, even pleasant; to give,
at least wisely, involves sweat and even tears."

One spectacularly sunny, chilly Saturday in March, I drove to Briarcliff Manor, New York, about an hour north of the city. The town has long been a haven for moneyed Manhattan commuters and their families, like many of the smaller communities in Westchester County—Pound Ridge, Waccabuc, Bedford, Purchase, and others. Briarcliff Manor, with a population of just over ten thousand, is the sixty-ninth wealthiest ZIP code in the country. The median household income is $164,093, the average home value is $908,492, and the ten thousand residents are worth an average of $1,255,498 each.

A friend who lives in town supplied me with a list of streets to walk, nooks where the home values crept above the average thanks to a good view or proximity to the best schools, inside information I couldn't have gleaned from Google Maps. As my friend cruised the town in her mind, rattling off neighborhoods and landmarks, she mentioned offhand that Brooke Astor's home was nearby.

Armed with a map drawn on the back of an envelope, I set out into Briarcliff Manor. Beautiful town. Lots of trees, some horse farms, rolling hills, mammoth houses, white fences, stone walls. Before long, I found myself pulling into the driveway leading to the approximately seventy acres that make up Holly Hill, Mrs. Astor's estate.

When her third husband, Vincent Astor, died in 1959, after less than six years of marriage, he left his fortune—some $135 million from his family's fur-trading and real estate businesses—to his wife and to his foundation. That's about $750 million in today's dollars. About half of it kept his widow wealthy for the rest of her days, and the other half endowed a philanthropic foundation that would spread hundreds of millions of dollars to people and institutions in New York City's five boroughs during her lifetime. Mrs. Astor decided early on in her stewardship of the foundation that because the Astors had amassed their fortune in the city, it should be given away there too.

A high stone wall hems in Holly Hill, and the house itself is not visible from the road. There was a gate, of course, and it happened to be open. Still, I parked just outside the gate, because a security guard was sitting in a car just inside. I got out and walked over to his car, and he popped out. I told him about my project and asked if anybody happened to be home. He shook his head and paused for a moment.

"It's . . . not a good time," he said with a weary politeness.

"Oh, I'm sorry," I said. "No problem."

"Yes, it's really not a good time at all." Now he even sounded forlorn.

I thanked him and wondered to myself if anything was wrong. Mrs. Astor was very old and had recently been at the center of a public battle over her fortune and her health. The previous year, New York City's newspapers were ablaze for weeks with the story that Mrs. Astor's son, Anthony Marshall, had allegedly been stripping his mother of her fortune—ceding her property in Maine to himself, selling her most cherished works of art, paying himself millions of dollars a year in salary as her caregiver, denying her medicine and the company of her beloved dogs, and forcing her to sleep on a urine-stained couch in her Park Avenue apartment. Marshall's son, Philip, sued his father and eventually wrested control of Mrs. Astor's estate from him. It was a highly undignified coda to the life of a woman who was not only rich but also, according to many who knew her, gracious, generous, funny, wicked, irreverent, and loved.

I wondered, as I drove away, what I would have learned from Mrs. Astor. She did not earn her money, of course—unless you count being married to Vincent Astor, by most accounts a rather unpleasant, controlling man. But she presided over her fortune as if she had personally sweated for every penny, like a young girl with a piggy bank full of babysitting money. Her style of philanthropy—and it comes in many styles—was to give relatively small amounts as seed money to causes that had next to nothing. She didn't control billions of dollars, like the Ford or Carnegie foundations do, but often those much larger charities would follow her lead once she had given a particular cause her stamp of approval—they relied on her as a kind of screener. In *The Last Mrs. Astor,* an entertaining and nuanced biography, Frances Kiernan cites a landmark 1972 study of American philanthropy by Waldeman Nielson called *The Big Foundations.* In it, the Vincent Astor Foundation was heralded as a model of efficiency, running on a thin budget and employing only three people who worked out of a small office in an unremarkable building. Mrs. Astor may have been fantastically wealthy, but she had managed to convince herself that there was no room for frittering away so much as a penny.

I did not get to meet her that day in March, but I believe I've come to understand one of the keys to her success: humility. Yes, she enjoyed throwing lavish dinner parties for presidents and moguls, but she never, ever saw herself as being a better person than the hundreds of thousands of poor people she helped. She rarely gave money to a place she had not personally visited and investigated, always dressed in a hat and white gloves. This is perhaps why those larger foundations felt comfortable that if Brooke Astor had decided a cause was worthy, the cause was indeed worthy. "We go and we see," she often said. "We never give to anything we don't see."

In 1967, Robert Kennedy, then the freshman senator from New York, spearheaded a community development project in Bedford-Stuyvesant, a once-glorious neighborhood in Brooklyn that had become run-down and dangerous. It was a bold undertaking requiring the participation and agreement of every resident of a certain two-block stretch. As usual, Mrs. Astor led the way by providing $1 million in seed money, to be followed by larger grants from the likes of the Ford Foundation. But before her grant went through, Mrs. Astor wanted to see the neighborhood herself. She wanted to find out personally whether each and every resident supported the program that would so radically transform their neighborhood. In *The Last Mrs. Astor*, Kiernan quotes Frank Thomas, the project's director:

> She came out to some of those meetings in the homes of people in the neighborhood. People were blown away by her. Well, even then you know she dressed the same wherever she happened to be going. It brought a style and level of quality that was very arresting and connected with the way that people dressed on Sundays when they went to church. The hat. The gloves. All of that. It connects. There was a resonance. She

would sit in the living room of people, and they would be talking about what was happening on their blocks. And she was very, very curious.

Nothing in Vincent Astor's will, as I understand it, demanded that his widow devote her life to carefully managing his foundation and thoughtfully disbursing it to worthy causes. She could have hired a director and gone about spending her half of the money, making token appearances at ribbon-cutting ceremonies and charity galas. Instead, she was humbled by the responsibility. Kiernan quotes Mrs. Astor's confidant Louis Auchincloss, who wrote of his good friend, "To spend is easy, even pleasant; to give, at least wisely, involves sweat and even tears."

If I had met Mrs. Astor at Holly Hill that day, I might not have learned much. She was old and fragile. But even a few years earlier, she might have told me that money is simply a tool—to make a good life and to make other lives good. I think she would have said that money is something we should be slightly in awe of, something we should respect. I think she was humble enough that she would have told me that she was no queen—maybe not even the city's first lady, as she was often called—but a woman who could never fulfill all of her philanthropic goals, even though she tried and tried, almost every day, to come close.

That night, when I got home, I went on the Internet to investigate the apparent poor timing of my attempt to visit her. It turns out she was celebrating her birthday—a few friends and family members had come by. She was 105. Four and a half months later, she died.

Understand Your Limitations

....

"Acting? I was too short. I was playing seventeen-year-olds when I was
almost thirty, so I said, 'Come on, you're never going to be a leading man.' "

....

There is another kind of humility that can work in your favor:
understanding your limitations. On the same day Ted Kaplan
called me and told me about the fruit business, I knocked on a
door in Beverly Hills and was greeted by a man with a smile. His
thick white hair crowned a tan, lined face, and I guessed he was in
his late sixties. Don Cook was his name, and he lived in a large,
stately home with manicured grounds, north of Sunset Boulevard, where the home prices are as steep as the hills.

Cook explained that he was working upstairs on the computer—as I understood him, a man from the store had come to
help him set it up—but he took a few minutes to tell me how he
had ended up living way up here in the Hollywood Hills. (I think
I had wandered from 90210 into 90069.)

"I came out here to be an actor, like we all did," he said,
chuckling. "I trained at the Pasadena Playhouse. There were a
couple of guys there named Dustin Hoffman and Gene Hack-
man. I don't know what ever happened to them." For years, Cook
worked at it, taking whatever parts came along—most of them
for characters much younger than he. "Acting? I was too short. I
was playing seventeen-year-olds when I was almost thirty, so I
said, 'Come on, you're never going to be a leading man,' " he told
me, with a resigned smile.

I have friends who are actors or are trying to be actors, and
I know this: actors are passionate people—passionate, mostly,
about acting and devoted to succeeding at it despite the odds.

When I knocked on Cook's door, decades had passed since his decision to leave his acting career behind, and I'm sure the pangs of disappointment had long faded. Still, it couldn't have been easy at the time.

But he did stumble into a good situation because of it. Something gave him the idea that it might be fun to own a clothing store. He and a partner scrounged up loans of about $25,000, and in 1958 they opened up a men's shop called Ah Men in a twenty-foot storefront. "We went after the gay trade in West Hollywood, which worked out pretty well, business-wise," he said. Later, in the early 1970s, a corner building went up for sale across the street, near the corner of San Vicente and Santa Monica boulevards. "Against a lot of advice, I purchased it. It cost $375,000, which was a lot of money in that day. I had to borrow some money from my father for the down payment. And at the last minute the owner raised the down payment he was asking for by $15,000. They were trying to discourage me from buying it. They didn't think a men's clothing store would do very well there. But I went ahead. I've always done everything from the gut. And the business prospered."

Not only did the store make a profit, but buying that building turned out to be a generous consolation prize for Cook's heartbreaking decision to leave acting. A bank came along and offered to buy the building, but instead of selling it to them, Cook signed them as a rent-paying tenant. He later added Mrs. Fields, the cookie company. Recently, he said, rumors surfaced in Santa Monica of an ordinance that would raise the height limit on commercial buildings from three stories to seven, which would make Cook's asset even more lucrative because he could then add more commercial space.

Like Jeff Weisfeld, the Beverly Hills produce broker and professional home seller you met in chapter 3, Cook would be the first to tell you that he's no real estate genius. ("I could have bought the house next door here for $149,000 once," Cook said. "Now it's worth four million.") Instead he is what you might call a self-taught moneymaker: he knows himself, he know his limits and his limitations, and he seems to base every decision on an aggregate of what he's learned from all the previous decisions he's ever made. "I've done everything from the gut," he said. "I put some money in the stock market, and I regret every penny. I've had some pretty good offers on the building, but that building is kind of my outlet to be active, and it gives me something to do. I live as well as I want to. When I was little, seven of us shared a bathroom. Now I have five bathrooms for myself."

Don't Be a Slave to Plan A – It'll Prevent You from Seeing Plan B

"You can never be positive it's not all going to fall down around you."

Three thousand miles away from Don Cook, in the city where I live, I found another man who had dreamed of a career as an actor, only to decide that another pursuit was, I suppose, more realistic.

A note on the locale: The Upper East Side of Manhattan is not represented on ESRI's list of the top hundred most affluent ZIP codes in the country. How can that be, when apartments there can sell for $15 million and townhouses for more than $30 million? When elite prep schools are nestled among neighbors like Michael Bloomberg, Edgar Bronfman, and Ivana Trump? Where hamburgers go for sixteen dollars?

The answer is that the ZIP codes there stretch far to the east of Central Park—all the way to the East River, in fact, which means they include many square blocks of starter apartments for recent college graduates, tight two bedrooms for young families, a few shabby buildings here and there, and the occasional public housing. Which is to say that once you get away from the homes close to the park, it's basically a normal neighborhood.

But oh, those homes by Central Park. I spent an unusually warm winter Saturday traversing the blocks between Park and Fifth avenues, from Sixtieth Street to Ninety-third. Before we were married, my wife lived in 10021, on Seventy-third Street east of First Avenue, in the same ZIP code as power brokers and ladies who lunch. She was in a small, prewar one bedroom, perfect for her and her (small) Boston terrier, Sam. For part of the time she lived there, I worked at the *New York Observer,* a weekly newspaper that covers the machinations of Manhattan's power elite. At the time it was owned by Arthur Carter, a former investment banker and one of the Upper East Side's moneyed denizens. On the walk I took that Saturday, a half-dozen years later, I passed by what a real estate Web site had identified as Carter's $34 million townhouse. (I didn't knock.)

I had walked these streets before, going to and coming from Sarah's cozy apartment, walking to work at the *Observer,* seeing art at the Metropolitan Museum, going to restaurants with my parents when they came to visit. The overwhelming majority of Manhattan residential real estate consists of apartment buildings, but in this enclave, single-family homes—narrow structures that are typically four or five floors—line the streets, shaded by leafy trees with neat squares of soil around their trunks. The homes, bound to one another by thin membranes of mortar, form a solid wall of wealth on each block. The faces of the townhouses, varied though they can be in color and style, create a single, long facade, like a movie set; I began to imagine princes and tycoons and fashion designers milling around behind it in a manicured garden stretching the entire block, sipping Armagnac and setting up their children with one another.

Turns out that's not the case. When I started ringing doorbells, I found there were actual homes behind those front doors. The houses themselves are so compact that the ones on a single city block would probably take four or five suburban streets if they were spread out with yards, so I was able to cover more houses with fewer footsteps. I still mostly talked to intercoms, and conversations with intercoms, on the whole, rarely resulted in interviews. (Me, shouting through static into the box: "No, a *writer*. I'm doing a book about—I was wondering if you could tell me about how you came to live here. Do you have a minute to talk?" Them: Silent.) The neighborhood was slow going for me, but the cool thing was that I started to see it differently than I ever had. It was just houses, with people living inside—like anywhere else. The trendy boutiques and city buses and the swishy restaurants and taxis faded into a background blur; all I saw were the homes. I noticed the kind of everyday activity you don't see when you *live* in the city because you're walking by so quickly: people checking their mail and taking down Christmas lights from the bushes out front, kids kicking off their sneakers just inside the front door. Even though I had arrived via subway, not (as I did in other cities) by air and rental car, I felt like an out-of-towner, invading yet another unsuspecting neighborhood. One key difference was that no one looked at me funny for going door to door. It was, after all, New York, and in New York anything goes.

Just after sunset, with several miles behind me, I was making my way across East Ninety-third Street from Madison to Fifth Avenue when I saw that the wrought-iron gate in front of a five-story, turn-of-the-century brick townhouse was ajar. As a general rule, if a gate was open, I entered.

When I rang the buzzer, no one came to the door. Instead, a man's voice came over the intercom, asking who was there. *Not again,* I thought. I went through my spiel halfheartedly, assuming defeat. But after a long pause, the voice said, "Hang on."

A man in his forties (I guessed), who looked a little like Dick Cavett, answered the door. His name was Gary Munch, and he told me that he and his wife had just returned from their week-end house but that she would be glad to talk to me. "I'm watching football and drinking beer," he said. "But she's the smart one anyway."

Liz Munch was taking the ornaments off the fourteen-foot Christmas tree that just about flicked the ceiling in a second-floor room facing the street. She wore a green T-shirt, jeans, and purple moccasins. I sat in a chair next to one of the house's four working fireplaces, but the weather was too warm for a fire. A dachshund played with a squeaky toy near my feet. In a china cabinet behind me, commemorative Elvis Presley dishes lined the shelves. Near the fireplace, a guitar autographed by the Allman Brothers leaned next to another one signed by Little Steven Van Zandt. *This is the kind of stuff I would buy if I were rich,* I thought to myself.

Liz told me early in our conversation that her family had some money, which hadn't hurt. But as she spoke—about how she and Gary never dreamed they would live in a house like this, about how they got lucky in the real estate market, and about how cool it was that a Rockefeller and a hedge-fund manager (Bruce Kovner, number ninety-one on *Forbes*'s list of the four hundred richest Americans in 2007) lived on the same block—it became clear that not everything had been handed to her, that she and her husband did not feel entitled to live where they lived, five doors from Central Park.

In fact, it took a humbling decision by Gary to advance the Munches to their current situation: he gave up acting, just like Don Cook had in Los Angeles. "He really wanted to be on Broadway, but it didn't pan out," Liz said. Which left Gary wondering what his next career would be.

Gary had grown up in a family without much money. "They had very, very little and lived in a tiny little house. They did fine, and they didn't suffer, but they had their steak on Sunday, you know? His mother reused plastic bags," Liz told me, carefully laying an ornament in a box. "You can never be positive it's not all going to fall down around you. His parents never borrowed money. Gary learned the ethic of being careful."

That caution—and an acute understanding that complacency is detrimental to wealth building—led Gary to what has turned out to be his life's work: managing real estate. Liz's family's real estate, as a matter of fact.

"My grandfather had made real estate investments a gazillion years ago," she said. But as he grew older, her grandfather took to managing the properties mostly over the phone. He would call down to Florida to check in, be told that everything was A-okay, and then call again the next year and get the same report. As it turned out, the properties weren't always in as good condition as he was told.

"Gary realized that somebody needed to manage the properties. So he taught himself how to do it," Liz said, stopping to smile a little. "He says that acting has helped him with this. Since then he has, I think, sold off all the investments my grandfather made and invested in new properties."

Just then, Gary appeared in the doorway, beer in hand. Must have been halftime.

"What's she telling you?"

Liz answered, saying that she had been telling me the story of his clever career switch. Gary shrugged, humbly, and shuffled out of the room. I laughed to myself—I truly did—because there was something comic about his shrug, something a little histrionic about his departure. He might have made a good character actor. But Plan B seemed to be working out well.

Don't Be Afraid to Make Less Than Your Spouse

"It wasn't hard for me. I love coaching high school sports."

I met a guy in Sandy Springs, Georgia, just outside Atlanta, whose story was almost the inverse of Munch's. His name was Mike Amerson, and he coached high school sports. I know that sports are important in Georgia, and it was really none of my business, but it seemed impossible that Coach Amerson made enough from the school system to afford a lovely, new stone home in the seventy-seventh richest ZIP code in the United States, where the average house is valued at $806,263. I believe I blurted out that very sentiment, and Amerson laughed a little and explained that he had in fact eschewed two other lucrative careers in favor of coaching—and that his wife's salary as a physician at a hospital "does help out in terms of being able to afford this."

Amerson fits in to this chapter on humility precisely because he left those other jobs. He had spent a couple of years in medical school before deciding he didn't really want to be a doctor, no matter how highly paid he might be. Then, "I did computers for a while, did pretty well at that," he said. I took the phrase "did pretty well" to mean that he had made a killing. But his heart hadn't been in it, and instead of getting sucked in further, he walked away and grabbed a whistle.

It made me think of my brother Michael, who works as an investment banker. (I almost typed "who is an investment banker," but that's not who he *is*, it's what he *does*. A nuance of language, but important, I think.) He has a dream of opening a restaurant after he makes "enough" money on Wall Street. My initial concern about this plan was that it seems like a lot of smart people go to Wall Street with similar plans—make a million dollars, quit, and do what you love—but end up staying forever because the concept of "enough" keeps growing in their minds. Suddenly, you're making a million dollars a year—the magic number! quit!—but the next guy up is making $1.2 million. So you plan to stay just one more year, but then $1.4 million seems doable, so you figure, just one more year. But the other night, Mike whipped up a roast duck with chestnut stuffing that assured me the restaurant has not drifted irretrievably far from his thoughts.

Anyway, Amerson had made enough, and his wife brought in good money now. Still, I asked, was it hard to walk away from significant potential earnings? If he had stuck with med school or continued to "do well" in the computer business, couldn't they be living in a house twice as big? Amerson looked at me for a moment, maybe a little bewildered.

"It wasn't hard for me," he said. "I love coaching high school sports." And his ego had no objections.

Never Feel As If You're Too Successful to Sweat

·····

"Everybody just worked hard — really to a distraction, almost.
Working hard is all I know."

·····

In Gates Mills, Ohio, I met a fascinating couple who also felt they had "enough" money and decided to do what made them happy instead of what made them richer. Peter and Joanne Greisinger live in one of several houses on a sprawling farm just outside of Cleveland. It seemed miraculous to me that the Greisingers' land hadn't been subdivided into lots sprouting McMansions, but over the years the town of Gates Mills has heroically resisted development. (With a lot of activism and campaigning by the Greisingers, it turns out.)

Peter and Joanne weren't the first people I met at Moxahela Farm. Just inside the gate, I knocked on the door of a small cottage, one of several outbuildings stationed along the gray driveway that ran the length of a city block before winding back toward a towering Tudor estate house in the distance (belonging to Joseph Gorman, of the previous chapter). The door to the small cottage opened, and a stocky, black-haired man, wearing a blue sweatshirt, shorts, and tube socks and moccasins, appeared. He said his name was Michael DeCorpo. He welcomed me in, pushing aside the ironing board that was set up in the foyer, and showed me to a seat on the sofa near his good-looking husky, Smiff. "My wife works for the owner," he told me. I wasn't sure at the time what he meant by that (owner of what?), but I sat watching a Disney movie while DeCorpo called the Greisingers, who lived down the driveway in what he called "the glass mansion." All of this thoroughly confused me.

"Joanne, hi, it's Michael. Thank you for the brownies."

After a few minutes, DeCorpo hung up and told me it would be okay if I went down to the glass mansion and talked to Peter and Joanne. Peter's grandfather was the original owner of the property, he said. Still wondering about the Tudor mansion off in the distance, I made my way down a different driveway to Peter and Joanne's house, which was indeed made of glass and reminded me of a Philip Johnson structure. The architect was actually Robert A. Little, a mid-twentieth-century modernist who was an early champion of environmentally friendly design. I stepped down into a sunken driveway (or maybe it was a courtyard that happened to be outside the garage), and there was Peter Greisinger, waving to me from a floor-to-ceiling window next to the door.

For the next forty-five minutes or so, I sat with Joanne and Peter, whose grandfather had, in fact, been the original owner of what was now Moxahela Farm, and who had built the Tudor mansion. The Greisingers themselves were an unabashedly friendly, informal, and candid couple. They both wore green fleece sweatshirts, and Joanne sat on the floor. The place was decorated in the same style as some of the homes I'd seen during my college years in Vermont: rustic, homespun, comfortable. A Zenith television was tucked into a small wood cabinet, and there were indoor plants scattered about.

Peter is a documentary filmmaker whose work tells the stories of many a regular Joe—notably in a film called *Small Business My Way,* which illuminates the lives of small hotel owners, gas station proprietors, and other moms and pops. Greisinger Films, his company, adheres fiercely to his beliefs, many of which focus on ecological economics, the scientific examination of how human consumption intersects with the natural world. I have every confidence that his films are well made and worthy of attention, but from a financial perspective I had to assume that the movies didn't exactly pay the mortgage on the glass mansion. It probably didn't even have a mortgage.

"I'm old money and proud of it," Peter said with a chuckle. He had grown up on the property where we sat, with its fruit trees and small cadre of caretakers and employees. Later, in a follow-up conversation, I asked him why, with his inheritance, he wasn't sitting on a beach somewhere instead of making obscure documentaries about the environment and socioeconomics and engaging in community and environmental activism, which he and Joanne have done increasingly in recent years. He laughed before I finished my sentence.

"I have friends who ask me that. They tell me, 'You're unique. You're actually doing something,' " he said. "The honest answer to that is I would go nuts. The anxiety of doing nothing—it's just not how I was raised. I grew up with the Protestant work ethic, which has the guilt of not contributing associated with it. There's a lot to do in the world, and I've been given the opportunity to do what many people can't, to do these things I want to do."

I don't know if Greisinger would concede this, but there is much to be admired about the way he perceives his privileged upbringing. As a young boy, he was surrounded by people who took care of him and attended to the acreage that surrounded him. But instead of developing feelings of entitlement—"I don't have to do anything! Sweet!"—he learned to value hard work. He observed that the family's employees took pride in their jobs and that they seemed to live good lives. Sitting on a beach would not only be boring for Greisinger, it would also be, in a way, shameful.

"All the people around me were hardworking, wonderful people. Whether it was the full-time gardeners who managed the fruit trees and the vegetable gardens, the Swedish caretakers who lived in one of the homes up where the DeCorpos live—these were hardworking people. Spectacular people. There was a horseman who was an amusing but a tough, tough gentleman who had us mucking out stalls and cleaning up around the horses. Everybody just worked hard—really to a distraction, almost. Working hard is all I know."

Remember That You Are Not, Nor Will You Ever Be, a God or a Goddess

"So many times in my life when I got a door slammed in my face, I would go looking for another door."

The venture capital business is an industry of king makers—people who control vast sums of money that they can mete out at their discretion to wannabes who plead for it. And nowhere are there more VC dollars—or more pleading wannabes—than in Silicon Valley, in northern California. You can understand how a successful venture capitalist there might have an inflated opinion of his or her value to society, the world, the universe.

The ego of Heidi Roizen, whom I met in the mayor's house in Atherton, is not inflated at all. She is what you would call an unbelievably successful Silicon Valley entrepreneur and venture capitalist. But even that would be an understatement, really. At the time we met, she was a managing director at Mobius Venture Capital, a Palo Alto firm with investments in the tech industry of around $2 billion. As the vice chair of the National Venture Capital Association, she had once met with Alan Greenspan when he was the chairman of the Federal Reserve Board, and also with President George W. Bush. When she hosts parties at her home, extraordinary people show up, like Carly Fiorina, the erstwhile chairwoman of Hewlett-Packard; Scott McNealy, the cofounder of Sun Microsystems; and Tim Draper, a founder of Draper Fisher Jurvetson, the legendary venture capital firm.

"I ran my first business when I was twelve," she told me. "I put on puppet shows for kids' birthday parties. This was around 1971. I'd charge five dollars a show. By high school, I was doing six shows every weekend and charging thirty-five dollars a show." Based on that little anecdote, you might think Roizen was simply born with a talent for business and that that makes her fundamentally different from, say, you. But that assessment wouldn't be quite right. Sure, her story demonstrates an ability to turn a profit, but it doesn't get at the deeper root of her success: a humble nature that allows her to excel in an industry not known for its humble participants.

Roizen started out her adult career as an entrepreneur—the person on the other side of the table, pleading for money. One of her companies was an operation set up to market a breakthrough computer program her brother had developed, an innovative spreadsheet program that was a precursor to Lotus 1-2-3. Always one to roll up her sleeves, Roizen would spend her nights burning copies of the program onto floppy disks using the sole IBM computer in the Stanford University library at the time. Her scrappiness paid off. Before she even went looking for investors a few years later, her marketing company was bringing in $3 million a year, and it topped out at $15 million a year before she sold it.

Running her business, she came to understand for the first time the mind-set of a small businessperson. "When I was a CEO, people would say, 'You're so lucky you have the freedom of a

CEO.' But I had the least free job of anyone. Most people can walk into work and say, 'Hmm, do I like my job? Should I go do something else?' But as a CEO, you can't. If we were having a bad quarter or something, I'd look out at all those cars in the parking lot and think about all those mortgages and car payments, and I would think about how to make it worthwhile for them to come to work here every day."

It struck me as a particularly modest way to look at the job of leading. Instead of crowing about her success, she was speaking earnestly about the nobility of providing a livelihood for her employees. She wasn't saying "Woe is me; heavy lies the crown" or anything like that. For her, being a boss meant not that you were entitled to a limousine but that people depended on you. And the pressure of people depending on you was far greater, perhaps, than the pressures of getting a business off the ground in the first place. After all, if you fail at that stage, the only person affected is you.

As a celebrated venture capitalist working in the nerve center of her industry, Roizen refused to adopt the persona of a deity — even if that's how the parade of dreamers treated her when they won precious minutes of her time to pitch their big ideas. But I suspect that her approach to her work — low-key and tenacious — was precisely what allowed her to so ably pluck the ideas that eventually became lucrative. She understood that a venture capitalist who spends all day patting herself on the back for her most recent success is going to be too busy preening to unearth the next Facebook. In a way, she sees herself as the least important person in the equation.

"You have to have access to *other people*," she said. We were sitting in Atherton mayor Charles Marsala's living room, Roizen's voluminous Prada bag sitting next to her on the sofa. "And the only way to have access to people is to create it. I wanted to meet with a senior executive at Google a few weeks ago" — not the easiest meeting to get, even for someone like Roizen, apparently. "So I asked for an introduction from someone we both knew, and the executive took the meeting. I thought, Wow. When it came time for the meeting, I went in and basically asked him why he had agreed to see me, and he said, 'You spoke to my business school class in 1991.' So when people ask me why I spend so much time speaking to students at different schools, it's because you never know."

At Mobius, Roizen was known to indulge more than a few college kids and graduate students who asked her if she had time to hear about an idea over a cup of coffee. "More often than not, I said, 'What the hell?' You never know what you're going to learn from a grad student. I wish more kids like Mark Zuckerberg asked me to have a cup of coffee!" she said, referring to the youthful founder of Facebook.

You never know. That right there, in fact, is one of the most important phrases for anyone wondering whether it's time to set out on his or her own — to take a chance, to switch careers, to pursue a dream. You never know. It almost sounds simplistic, but no one ever said this was complicated.

Of course, implied in the phrase "you never know" is an understanding of possible failure. Losing, Roizen says, is no fun, but sometimes losing in the short-term is essential to winning later. When an investment failed, she never kicked herself or tried to erase the bad experience from memory. Rather, she slipped into the role of analyst, critiquing her decision making in the same way she dissects her performance after delivering one of her frequent talks to MBA students at Stanford and other schools. Instead of ignoring her shortcomings, she tried to understand them.

"After a talk, I spend a half hour telling my husband what went right or wrong," she said. "If I sit and think and talk out loud about what worked or didn't work, that becomes part of my psyche for how I figure out how to do the next lecture. I do the same thing in business."

Roizen told me that the song "18 Wheeler" by Pink is an important one on the soundtrack of her life. It's a sort of modern-day, slightly crass "I Will Survive." "It's a chick empowerment song. So many times in my life when I got a door slammed in my face, I would go looking for another door," Roizen said. These are not words that suggest pomposity or ego. Unfortunately, she didn't always see the same humility in the people who came to Mobius seeking an investment in their young business. Some of them didn't even have the courtesy to send a note thanking her for her time. Even though she wasn't meeting with people out of altruism, the thank-you note is a custom in the industry, one that shows, at the very least, that you have a selfish interest in maintaining a good relationship.

"For every thousand deals I looked at, I turned down nine hundred and ninety-eight. It's interesting to see how people respond to that rejection. They spend hours and hours working on a pitch, and then they can't spend thirty seconds to write a quick note to say thanks for listening to it," she said.

Roizen works hard to make sure that, despite growing up in America's wealthiest ZIP code, her children learn that a good businessperson is not prideful and values relationships—with the people she depends on and with the people who depend on her. Her daughter, Marleyna, once set up a stand and sold pumpkins in front of the house. "She and her friend made thirty-two dollars. At the end of the day I said, 'What about me?' And my daughter said, 'What do you mean?' I said, 'Me. I bought the seed. I lent you the backyard to grow the pumpkins.' So she and her friend thought about it and had a little discussion, and they gave me two dollars. One for the earth, one for the seeds."

The spirit of entrepreneurship that seems to pervade every corner of Atherton does rub off in good ways, Roizen told me. Once, doing grade school homework, Marleyna was playing around on a Web site when she let out a heavy sigh. When Roizen asked what was the matter, her daughter answered, "I just can't figure out what their business model is."

Roizen recalled another time, when at a young age Marleyna showed resourcefulness and a (humble) willingness to admit that plan A wasn't working. "We have these three chickens that I got so we could have fresh eggs," Roizen said. "Now my kids want to sell the eggs. Marleyna was once selling eggs out in front of the house. She wasn't getting much business, so she thought about her marketing and how to get people in. Her solution was to make a big sign that said 'Meet the chickens.' "

Marleyna will now get the chance to see her mother start a business of her own. In 2007 Roizen left Mobius to launch SkinnySongs, a company that produces workout music for women. The lyrics are all about losing weight and feeling better, and the lyricist is Roizen herself: *For months now, I've worked hard until yesterday / I went to the closet and pushed those 'fat clothes' away / I grabbed you—and I can't believe how it felt / To pull the zipper up, and buckle my belt! / Skinny jeans, skinny jeans, glad I kept you around / 'Cause tonight, my darlins, we're goin' out on the town.*

"It's scary, exciting, and fun to be an entrepreneur again," Roizen said. "Creating something from nothing is what drives me. This isn't some midlife crisis vanity project. I didn't cut a CD.

I came up with an idea that I thought was compelling. It wasn't like I was sitting around trying to start a company because I think anything I do will work. That can't be the goal in and of itself. I had an idea. I've hit that moment where even if I fail, I still need to do it."

Some people, of course, can remain absolutely arrogant for their entire careers and still make truckloads of money. Fine. Let them roll around in their cash. If they're lucky, it will keep multiplying. But the only way to make sure it does—or at least, to do everything you can—is to roll up your sleeves, swallow your pride, and keep working for it. Maybe fear lies beneath this humility, a fear of failure that makes it okay to work hard even when you're already successful.

A few months ago, I was helping my father carry an old, metal filing cabinet out to the garage to be thrown away. One of the drawers slid open, and a stack of worn, leather-bound ledger books spilled out onto the cement floor. We flipped through a few of them, and they turned out to be penny-for-penny logs of my parents' finances when they were first married. On page after page, their young lives were chronicled in financial transactions. This was back when most people wrote checks for even small purchases, so just about every dollar they spent was accounted for. We flipped through month after month, my father narrating as his memory touched down on the everyday moments that made up a young marriage more than three decades ago. A check for $150 to the University of Connecticut—"That was tuition for a whole semester of law school," he said. Another check for $20 to Master Charge, "our first credit card." One made out to Cash for, oddly, $1, Christmas Eve ("I don't have a clue about that one"). A week later, on New Year's Eve, $17.72 spent at the Highland Park Supermarket for a dinner party. Ten dollars a year to *Playboy* (I had no idea). Two hundred dollars for a second-hand motor for the '65 Volkswagen bug ("I put it in myself," my father said). Then the kids came: Twenty dollars cash on the day I was born ("probably to fill up the car with gas"). Months later, a check for $25.20 to General Bagless Diaper, a delivery service. Another for $5 to my mom's younger sister, Maura, for babysitting. The occasional $250 or $300 deposit for legal work my dad was doing on the side—house closings and the like. It was an amazing documentary of a life, told through money earned and spent.

That my parents even maintained these records and kept them all these years suggests that they share a few qualities of the billionaires of Atherton, the waterfront residents of Westport, and everyone else I met in America's richest neighborhoods. The people I met never miss a chance to go after something they want, because they know that the more information they have, the better prepared they are to seize opportunities. If you don't have a dollar, you can't jump on the bus. They know that casual interest in their life's work or their own finances won't lead to much. They understand that a risky opportunity becomes less risky the more you learn about it. And they know that when a risk pays off, it's not dumb luck.

The ledger books were the meticulous accounts of careful spenders, people with no money to spare. In the many years since, my parents have done very well and no longer need to budget so diligently for every tank of gas or to chronicle every check cashed. But here's the thing: they still do. Every month, at the kitchen table, the current log comes out of the mahogany flip-top desk, and every penny is accounted for. They could probably afford to skip it once in a while, assured that everything would be okay. They could, but they don't. Doing that would be a little arrogant. And they've had too many good ideas, worked too hard, and taken enough risks to ever let complacency get in the way of their success and happiness.

TOP 100 WEALTHIEST ZIP CODES IN AMERICA

RANKED BY WEALTH INDICATORS FROM ESRI

ESRI Wealth Rank	5-Digit ZIP Code	Post Office Name	State	2007 Population	2007 Median Household Income	2007 Median Age	2007 Average Net Worth	2007 Median Disposable Income	2007 Average Home Value
1	94027	Atherton	CA	7,279	$226,414	45.4	$1,505,508	$156,551	$1,236,572
2	22067	Greenway	VA	228	$191,428	50.4	$1,771,852	$126,871	$1,141,438
3	94028	Portola Valley	CA	6,637	$209,274	46.3	$1,494,566	$147,620	$1,218,345
4	94022	Los Altos	CA	18,870	$191,519	47.3	$1,467,177	$131,114	$1,207,167
5	92067	Rancho Santa Fe	CA	3,411	$218,982	46.4	$1,556,055	$155,050	$1,244,824
6	60043	Kenilworth	IL	2,517	$219,051	41.5	$1,415,676	$151,739	$1,104,480
7	10577	Purchase	NY	4,076	$186,493	24.4	$1,409,646	$114,529	$1,112,650
8	22066	Great Falls	VA	18,031	$202,451	41.0	$1,439,586	$132,891	$1,054,545
9	19035	Gladwyne	PA	4,168	$205,945	51.3	$1,526,827	$155,364	$999,738
10	02493	Weston	MA	11,573	$209,208	41.9	$1,393,673	$137,100	$1,066,868
11	07976	New Vernon	NJ	630	$151,415	48.8	$1,517,034	$100,916	$1,102,113
12	10576	Pound Ridge	NY	5,148	$182,697	42.1	$1,410,765	$111,811	$1,070,355
13	10518	Cross River	NY	521	$185,272	38.2	$1,392,187	$113,401	$925,257
14	10514	Chappaqua	NY	12,775	$201,287	38.8	$1,353,291	$117,750	$998,226
15	94920	Belvedere Tiburon	CA	12,206	$150,433	47.5	$1,380,828	$107,096	$1,195,904
16	06883	Weston	CT	10,184	$182,629	39.7	$1,355,728	$120,227	$1,075,336
17	11568	Old Westbury	NY	3,860	$191,303	35.3	$1,341,146	$115,761	$1,157,284
18	07021	Essex Fells	NJ	2,071	$189,380	41.5	$1,348,338	$127,554	$1,035,571
19	10526	Goldens Bridge	NY	2,043	$165,262	39.3	$1,401,764	$105,090	$837,540
20	10546	Millwood	NY	1,028	$178,505	39.2	$1,397,723	$111,995	$941,962
21	07078	Short Hills	NJ	12,845	$218,398	39.7	$1,276,165	$151,890	$1,110,364
22	06840	New Canaan	CT	19,920	$185,491	40.9	$1,289,795	$119,419	$1,125,722
23	19085	Villanova	PA	9,380	$188,827	22.2	$1,409,358	$140,304	$941,240
24	06612	Easton	CT	7,537	$154,416	41.9	$1,429,018	$103,902	$915,520
25	60022	Glencoe	IL	8,340	$198,614	42.8	$1,376,595	$127,663	$954,652
26	01773	Lincoln	MA	5,199	$148,334	45.9	$1,415,094	$100,759	$958,666

ESRI Wealth Rank	5-Digit ZIP Code	Post Office Name	State	2007 Population	2007 Median Household Income	2007 Median Age	2007 Average Net Worth	2007 Median Disposable Income	2007 Average Home Value
27	07046	Mountain Lakes	NJ	4,353	$183,048	41.2	$1,293,371	$122,936	$979,585
28	07620	Alpine	NJ	2,280	$169,440	43.3	$1,378,459	$113,300	$1,153,221
29	10597	Waccabuc	NY	987	$164,341	40.6	$1,336,806	$105,997	$915,655
30	60045	Lake Forest	IL	23,538	$164,906	42.0	$1,374,609	$111,703	$929,715
31	22039	Fairfax Station	VA	19,655	$184,052	43.5	$1,347,768	$123,486	$926,599
32	10504	Armonk	NY	7,691	$161,140	40.5	$1,352,361	$103,037	$1,098,618
33	06897	Wilton	CT	17,942	$175,535	40.6	$1,293,845	$116,065	$1,002,155
34	11765	Mill Neck	NY	468	$166,457	43.2	$1,299,725	$106,002	$1,089,552
35	95070	Saratoga	CA	32,308	$179,963	45.1	$1,312,743	$124,921	$1,192,465
36	90077	Los Angeles	CA	9,350	$200,544	45.0	$1,331,615	$135,245	$1,218,334
37	21153	Stevenson	MD	431	$141,764	46.8	$1,488,797	$99,297	$871,069
38	10506	Bedford	NY	5,408	$184,845	39.4	$1,260,144	$113,935	$1,078,155
39	92694	Ladera Ranch	CA	2,485	$141,614	48.1	$1,399,553	$102,730	$813,082
40	92091	Rancho Santa Fe	CA	4,162	$174,096	47.3	$1,437,361	$119,690	$992,723
41	06820	Darien	CT	20,763	$182,739	38.4	$1,253,795	$118,952	$1,054,243
42	94507	Alamo	CA	15,261	$172,397	44.6	$1,356,594	$120,117	$1,191,295
43	06880	Westport	CT	26,937	$157,087	42.3	$1,278,975	$105,492	$1,032,553
44	11797	Woodbury	NY	9,629	$163,703	45.3	$1,366,154	$104,440	$1,016,231
45	02468	Waban	MA	5,643	$176,384	45.0	$1,315,793	$114,715	$969,564
46	11576	Roslyn	NY	13,555	$162,486	44.8	$1,348,323	$104,241	$1,004,271
47	94024	Los Altos	CA	22,062	$170,507	45.3	$1,272,347	$119,460	$1,203,724
48	20854	Potomac	MD	51,793	$172,442	43.7	$1,279,043	$119,707	$998,634
49	90272	Pacific Palisades	CA	24,144	$161,362	44.7	$1,369,850	$114,359	$1,177,762
50	11724	Cold Spring Harbor	NY	2,899	$162,431	39.8	$1,363,006	$103,096	$1,042,601
51	07931	Far Hills	NJ	4,399	$155,261	41.7	$1,258,421	$104,721	$936,131
52	22101	McLean	VA	28,579	$161,886	45.0	$1,295,581	$109,210	$920,849
53	06831	Greenwich	CT	15,720	$158,051	42.8	$1,218,819	$106,317	$1,069,568
54	11030	Manhasset	NY	17,578	$165,125	43.2	$1,296,166	$105,238	$1,136,839
55	94506	Danville	CA	32,353	$194,022	39.7	$1,211,724	$134,156	$1,174,754
56	01921	Boxford	MA	8,542	$158,649	42.4	$1,370,542	$107,007	$764,969
57	98039	Medina	WA	3,041	$174,294	42.5	$1,349,511	$128,702	$1,126,264
58	28274	Charlotte	NC	404	$125,000	31.1	$1,378,001	$100,000	$677,273
59	95030	Los Gatos	CA	12,810	$156,928	44.1	$1,207,887	$110,503	$1,199,529
60	94528	Diablo	CA	754	$152,607	44.6	$1,224,122	$107,379	$1,073,548
61	90274	Palos Verdes Peninsula	CA	26,089	$151,779	47.7	$1,356,229	$108,320	$1,203,644
62	06853	Norwalk	CT	3,395	$148,631	42.9	$1,234,848	$102,133	$955,677
63	85253	Paradise Valley	AZ	18,890	$157,478	46.3	$1,356,956	$110,949	$1,070,460
64	90210	Beverly Hills	CA	23,949	$149,195	46.4	$1,250,635	$107,802	$1,216,175

ESRI Wealth Rank	5-Digit ZIP Code	Post Office Name	State	2007 Population	2007 Median Household Income	2007 Median Age	2007 Average Net Worth	2007 Median Disposable Income	2007 Average Home Value
65	94563	Orinda	CA	18,082	$145,188	47.7	$1,299,762	$104,288	$1,154,159
66	10583	Scarsdale	NY	38,244	$159,637	41.5	$1,205,544	$102,781	$891,897
67	01770	Sherborn	MA	4,200	$166,271	42.6	$1,277,891	$110,381	$930,377
68	07458	Saddle River	NJ	11,363	$166,336	41.5	$1,263,882	$112,513	$1,141,484
69	10510	Briarcliff Manor	NY	10,114	$164,093	39.6	$1,255,498	$104,196	$908,492
70	90402	Santa Monica	CA	12,693	$148,789	44.9	$1,266,902	$106,913	$1,199,130
71	45228	Cincinnati	OH	468	$138,631	42.6	$1,256,884	$94,398	$491,503
72	20816	Bethesda	MD	15,798	$152,038	44.7	$1,278,605	$106,933	$973,768
73	07945	Mendham	NJ	9,805	$158,244	42.5	$1,282,691	$106,680	$926,576
74	01776	Sudbury	MA	17,009	$162,223	40.4	$1,259,072	$109,197	$808,720
75	07417	Franklin Lakes	NJ	10,892	$167,985	41.0	$1,230,149	$112,874	$1,100,151
76	33480	Palm Beach	FL	11,276	$103,790	65.7	$1,386,837	$80,016	$838,024
77	30327	Atlanta	GA	22,851	$142,024	41.6	$1,219,205	$101,736	$806,263
78	60093	Winnetka	IL	19,484	$164,786	42.2	$1,228,826	$111,688	$910,274
79	07930	Chester	NJ	9,038	$147,588	40.2	$1,270,191	$100,158	$864,236
80	10590	South Salem	NY	7,186	$138,920	41.8	$1,232,685	$90,384	$806,266
81	20817	Bethesda	MD	33,063	$149,059	44.9	$1,239,181	$105,249	$930,493
82	10538	Larchmont	NY	16,439	$156,105	39.2	$1,149,249	$100,911	$934,846
83	06903	Stamford	CT	14,733	$152,102	42.1	$1,194,340	$102,971	$1,035,772
84	02030	Dover	MA	5,717	$196,983	38.8	$1,180,281	$123,928	$1,059,552
85	10580	Rye	NY	17,748	$150,052	39.3	$1,143,042	$97,481	$980,955
86	11024	Great Neck	NY	8,073	$145,495	38.1	$1,252,695	$94,751	$1,052,240
87	07632	Englewood Cliffs	NJ	5,246	$141,980	45.7	$1,227,535	$97,791	$1,040,908
88	63124	Saint Louis	MO	9,579	$116,529	48.7	$1,309,829	$83,817	$800,707
89	31411	Savannah	GA	8,025	$121,722	64.6	$1,371,672	$90,375	$651,102
90	07934	Gladstone	NJ	1,567	$128,240	41.1	$1,169,186	$88,476	$938,611
91	10502	Ardsley	NY	5,703	$144,132	44.9	$1,236,909	$92,244	$782,352
92	92603	Irvine	CA	10,668	$139,257	43.8	$1,297,848	$101,153	$1,124,614
93	60523	Oak Brook	IL	9,945	$119,381	55.6	$1,359,711	$83,995	$792,275
94	33921	Boca Grande	FL	1,452	$139,493	63.4	$1,260,600	$103,439	$1,103,392
95	10804	New Rochelle	NY	14,457	$158,277	42.6	$1,187,224	$102,578	$859,532
96	44040	Gates Mills	OH	3,242	$132,297	47.9	$1,351,184	$93,309	$556,827
97	21738	Glenwood	MD	2,493	$141,614	41.6	$1,234,089	$98,933	$832,307
98	01742	Concord	MA	17,535	$131,668	43.9	$1,250,933	$87,364	$839,120
99	08558	Skillman	NJ	7,626	$160,912	39.7	$1,130,359	$108,967	$752,441
100	20818	Cabin John	MD	1,764	$139,423	44.5	$1,140,562	$95,422	$924,468

ZIP Codes: This table lists, in rank order, the 100 wealthiest ZIP Codes in the United States. ZIP Codes with a population of less than 100 are eliminated from the list. The wealthiest places or ZIP Codes are commonly identified by household income. ESRI's list of the wealthiest areas is compiled from a number of indicators of affluence that include average household income and average net worth. Wealth is more than above-average household income. The concept of wealth also includes the value of material possessions and resources. ESRI captures both income and the accumulation of substantial wealth, or the abundance of possessions and resources, in its identification of the country's wealthiest areas. Top ranks reflect both accumulated wealth and the rate of increase in wealth as measured by current income.

ACKNOWLEDGMENTS

My parents, John and Sheila D'Agostino, are the hardest-working people I know, and the wisest. They taught me everything, including the value of a dollar and, more important, that a dollar means nothing without loved ones to spend it on.

One obvious group I need to thank heartily are the people around the country who agreed to be interviewed for this book. Without their generous contributions of time, knowledge, and candor, I would have been nowhere.

I didn't know the first thing about how to turn this idea into a book, so I sought the help of Jean Chatzky. She never hesitated to share her good advice and hard-won wisdom.

I am grateful to Carol Dweck and Jason Zweig, and also to Stephen Garcia, for their insights and their willingness to contribute their expertise to this project. Donna Fancher at ESRI was the cheerful and generous compiler of the statistical information about each ZIP code that appears on the master list that ESRI created exclusively for me.

Eric Schurenberg and Craig Matters let me run with this idea in the first place. I was working at *Money* when I initially went door knocking; Eric green-lighted the story that eventually ran (in which some of the people in this book appeared), and

Craig edited it with his characteristic skepticism, deftness, and passion.

My supremely cool-headed editor at Little, Brown, Tracy Behar, understood this book from the beginning and helped me corral my travels into a narrative with some cogency and utility. Richard Pine, my peerless agent, was a wise, patient answerer of questions and a trusted partner in bringing this book to existence. Marie Salter, the sharpest of copyeditors, made every page better.

Peter and Katie Heimbold gave me invaluable encouragement from start to finish, and Kendall and Tory Hamilton lent enthusiastic support and an idyllic place to work. Bill Shapiro and Jon Gluck, like Kendall, taught me a lot about how to write this book before I ever had the idea to do it, and I'll always be grateful to the three of them. Tom Chiarella was a patient, honest sounding board and editor.

Many other people helped in innumerable and essential ways: Lindsay and Rett Coluccio, Eloise Bune D'Agostino, Margo Estrada, Yvonne Fisher, David Granger, John Kenney, Jed and Andy Moran, Charles and Monika Heimbold, and Chad and Sybil. Also Cal Fussman and Mike Sager, for the words of wisdom; Amanda Gengler and Chris Berend, for the snap research; and Josh Paul and Steve Fusco, for making me look presentable.

My travels around the country would have been far less enjoyable (and more expensive) were it not for the generous hospitality of Maura, Tank, Harry and Savannah Phillips; Matt Baker and Carly Vynne; Joe and Elizabeth Carpenter; Jason and Jessica Graham; Andrew and Kate Ritter; Arlene Winnick on behalf of Raffles L'Ermitage; and Scott Zdanis. (And thanks also to the late, great, Tom Fisher.) Justin Racz accompanied me to Austin on a whim and made a fun trip a lot more fun. I received invaluable local knowledge from Tom and Mary Ritter, Earl Willens, and a nice fellow at the BP station somewhere near Sandy Springs, Georgia. A big thanks also to Susan Hosmer of Bullfrog and Baum for introducing me to the generous hospitality of others.

Several people heroically read all or part of this book at various stages of progress, and each of them helped the end result in important ways, small and large—my brother, Michael D'Agostino, especially, and also Kendall Hamilton, David Katz, Rachael Dorsey McGowen, and John Moran.

Most of all, I want to thank my wife, Sarah, for all the notes in my suitcase, for reading every word as fast as I could write it, and for supporting me in more ways than she knows; and John Hudson, for always smiling when I walked in the door.

Ryan D'Agostino is an editor at *Esquire* magazine. His work has appeared in *The New Yorker, Money, New York,* and other publications. He lives in New York City with his family.